The Everspace: Utilizing the Power of God a...
Neuroscience to Create Stillness Within.

****

****

Want Free Books?

I'm giving away three free books if you are interested. These books have been highly influential in my development as a human being and all of them come in kindle format for your convenience. Type the following link in your browser and please consider signing up at http://downloadingdaily.com/books/three-free-books/

****

Also By Chris:

The Death Of the Diet

1

Table of Contents

3

For my Father, Carl

Introduction

I can remember it vividly. I was 8 or 9 years old and I was upset about something walking into the back door of my garage. I was pulling on my golden hair, yelling at God, and asking Him why He was doing this to me. I was angry, confused, but actually talking to God like I knew Him. I went to Catholic school sure, but that wasn't what this was about. I wasn't trying to do what someone else told me to do. It was instinctual, or intuitive.
Just like when a child asks where babies come from, I was too young to understand the answer to my question, so no solution was given. I realized I was on my own with this one and my attention soon turned back to playing.

As I grew up, my relationship with God slipped in and out of focus. I found church to be a waste, so when I was confirmed, I told my parents I was going, and then went and played basketball somewhere.

Then I became self-righteous. When people inquired about my religion, I told them God never put the books in my hand that made me smarter; I did all of it on my own.

In my early 20's I became agnostic. I liked the idea of not labeling anything, but believing that there may be a higher power that looks over us all and helps us when we are ready to be helped. It comforted me.

Late in my 20's I was introduced to Hafiz and Rumi, and fell in love with their descriptions of the Beloved, or "Friend" as they called him (or her). The idea that God could be seen everywhere and in everything, that we are all interconnected, appealed to me.

All I had to do was love everyone, and treat them how I wanted to be treated, and my life would turn out ok.

Sounds easy enough.

As I dug deeper and deeper into the spirituality of things a lot of questions started to come up. Books by Don Miguel Ruiz, Eckhart Tolle, and Dr. Wayne Dyer shed some light for me, but there was one question I just couldn't shake and that was, "What principles do I have to have to enter this space you guys are in?"

While most people are chasing material things to garner success, success for me is determined by a calm inner being. I was tired of the psychological unrest I felt in situations I knew didn't warrant it. To me, there is no greater dysfunction than thinking or feeling what you are doing isn't right, but going ahead and doing it anyway. I knew the answers were out there, I just didn't understand why I wasn't decoding it all.

Consciousness is an amazing aspect of our existence that has been debated upon for years. Upon reflecting, I had held my own internal debates on the matter. My ultimate question that I unconsciously was posing to myself was do I use the principles of science to guide me, or religion? For instance, in October of 2015 I visited the town of Assisi, Italy and became aware of the song St. Francis created in the year 1225 called Canticle of the Creatures. In it St. Francis speaks as if everything from the sun to the animals to even the weather having a soul. In philosophy this is called panpsychism; the belief that the mind and soul is a universal and primordial feature of all things. All

7

things? When was the last time you looked at your dining room table as having a mind, and/or soul? Lets back up for a second.

In 2011 I came across a book called The Field written by Lynne McTaggart and BAM! There it was. This was what I was searching for. Proof of a sort of uber consciousness, or extreme connectedness that we all share. Scientists call it the Zero Point Field. Einstein knew about it and said, "The Field is the only thing that's real, and all things are contained therein." My curiosity grew. The book was mind blowing and it showed that science was on to this same altruistic virtue St. Francis was trying to pitch to us almost 800 years ago. We are all connected by some conscious fabric that is invisible unless you allow it in your life. In the case of science, all it takes is measurement.

We're not going to stop there though. A new theory in neuroscience is suggesting that consciousness can be measured in all things and is as consistent as gravity. It's called Integration Information Theory (IIT) and treats consciousness as an intrinsic, fundamental property of reality.

Forgive me for being a little Star Wars – ISH. We flashed back, and then flashed back further, then flashed forward, and now we're flashing back again. That song that St. Francis wrote wasn't actually written. Legend has it that he was under such physical pain and duress that he actually dictated it. It was at the point where his entire physical body was failing, and he succumbed to blindness that his consciousness was at it's sharpest.

Luckily, I am not advocating a removal of sensory organs

to obtain the same peacefulness Francis acquired before his death. Rather than pitch knowledge versus faith, I'm trying to convince you that to be the person you want, and to get the most you can from your life it takes a firm grasp of both to make this happen.

For instance, our subconscious/unconscious mind can process nearly 11 million pieces of information a second compared to 40 with the conscious mind (1). Does this fact help both believers and non-believers alike? I believe it does. When Jesus was dying on the cross he said, "Forgive them Father, for they know not what they do." In this he was talking of their ego. The soldiers knew exactly what they were doing to Jesus; the problem was they thought it was real. That's the ever-illusive ego for you. Can a better understanding of the ego help a non-church goer, as well as a churchgoer live a better, more productive life? I'm compelled to say - sure.

I'm convinced that the reason why most of us do not have what we want, or live the life we love is because we allow too many distractions in our daily life. We have shiny object syndrome. Sensory overload. We place value on the invaluable which causes us to operate in another realm other than the here and now. It's like a lawyer hanging out in an auto-body shop to learn more about law. We get notifications from Facebook, Twitter, Pinterest, or our e-mail every minute on the hour. If you can't even concentrate on improving your work because of these distractions, how will you concentrate on improving your life?

We then incur mountains of borrowed money or "debt" to buy things we don't need, and when it all goes bust, the banks tell us we actually have less than nothing. In return, our psyche becomes broken. The Native Americans called this Wetiko. It was considered a mental illness that some tribe members exhibited by taking more than they needed. They saw this illness in white people when they started inhabiting North America. Gone is the little house on the prairie and in comes the world of genetically modified food, and smartphones that think for you. It's no wonder that as corporations humanize our food and possessions, we start to feel less and less human.

When you quiet your life, quiet your mind, begin to live with integrity, and learn how to communicate with what your spirit is after, this beautiful space I call The Everspace comes alive inside of you. It becomes accessible through your own intuition. It's a place of connectedness, abundance and love through which all life operates out of. The staggering fact is that you actually won't be learning anything; it will be you remembering through awareness.

Some of the ideas in this book can be considered utopian. Other ideas in this book can be characterized as visionary. Like you'll find out, what you tend to believe or not believe comes down to your perspective on these things.
As human beings we create our world, create our happiness, and create our misery by how we think and what we focus on. This book is aimed at turning your focus on the positive energy of the world, and connecting with emotions that are feelings, not just thoughts because thinking as we will find out is the boobie prize presented to everyone in life. When you transcend thinking is where the difference occurs.

The single biggest assumption we can make is that change isn't going to occur overnight. Good things take time to develop. Gold requires years of heat, and diamonds take years of pressure, yet it's the rarity of both that make them valuable. In the end this book is about love, or the rarity of true love, for yourself, your partner, your neighbor, and most importantly life.

When you love people, they don't always love you back and that's ok, but I guarantee that if you love life, life will always love you back. Love requires one simple skill; the ability to give more than you receive, and that is what makes this idea so out of reach at the current moment because the current generation is all about process and retrieval. More going in, less coming out. More interaction with screens and keyboards, less with people and nature. Not everyone has the ability to make millions of dollars, but everyone does have the ability to serve another human being, and when it is done without expectation of receiving something in return it places value on that life. We need to value that value, rather than seeing it as an empty investment, and we need to view it as the most enriching of all virtues. This is very hard.

Africa, a so-called third-world continent, known for its frequent uprisings, apartheid, and genocides is now leading the way with an ethical concept known as Ubuntu. Notice I said concept, not word. Archbishop Desmond Tutu refers to Ubuntu as our interconnectedness. "You can't be human all by yourself, and when you have this quality, Ubuntu, you are known for your generosity. We think of ourselves far too frequently as just individuals, separated from one another, whereas you are connected and what you do affects the whole world. When you do well, it spreads out; it is for the whole of humanity. A person with Ubuntu is open and available to others, affirming of others, does not feel threatened that others are able and good, based from a proper self-assurance that comes from knowing that he or she belongs in a greater whole and is diminished when others are humiliated or diminished, when others are tortured or oppressed (2)".

I believe Ubuntu helps us to stop seeing love as just a word and brings it back to when it was an ethically responsible concept. Today we love our iPhones, our clothes, our video games, our sports, our movies, we love ice cream, we love restaurants, and the list goes on and on. So, when we say we love another human being the meaning is actually diminished.

When I hear people say they love these things I'm reminded of a scene in Anchorman with Brick Tamland standing in Ron Burgundy's office saying, "I love lamp, I love carpet" in complete monotone. Whether it's the love of a family member, or the love of a significant other, our concept of love should be an unconditional surrender of the selfish pursuit of happiness. Other people, and especially material things should not be responsible for making us happy. Besides, true love is expressed when we are deeply and emotionally affected by another person's happiness, not our own. When we institute this concept of love, life uncovers the rarest of all symbiotic balances in the Universe – by helping others, we are actually helping ourselves.

My hope is that at the end of this book, those of you who struggle to have a sense of God in your life will develop one applicable to your values, beliefs, meaning and understanding of the world and what your mission is. For those of you who do have a sense of faith, I hope the science helps you develop both personally and professionally in times when your faith is tested. My very best to all of you on your respective journeys.

CK - Johannesburg, South Africa
November 2016

References:
1. Coyle, D. (2009). The Talent Code: Greatness Isn't Born. It's Grown. Here's How. Bantam Dell, New York, New York.
2. I am, because of you: Further reading on Ubuntu. (2014). Retrieved December 08, 2016, from http://blog.ted.com/further-reading-on-ubuntu/

The World Is His,

*Who Can See Through Its
Pretension....*

*See It to Be A lie, and You Have
Already Dealt It*

Its Mortal Blow.

-Ralph Waldo Emerson

EverLesson 1: It's All About Perspective

"We can complain that rose bushes have thorns, or we can rejoice that thorn bushes have roses."

-Abraham Lincoln

"Adults keep asking children what they want to be when they grow up 'cause they're looking for ideas."

-Paula Poundstone

Paris, France

A Tale of Two Citizens

There is no doubt we are all stuck deep in the doo doo of personality. We all think we are someone special. We create our worlds every day, yet we are not the creator. Our drama is so important to us and, yet there are infinitely more important things going on in the universe than Khloe breaking up with Lamar. If you think you're bigger than an ant, I'd have to disagree. An ant knows its purpose in life. What is yours?

Let's pretend we are in the Wild Wild West. You found a nice little piece of land next to a beautiful river. The mountains aren't too far away when you need to hunt, or gather food. The pasture's soil is very fertile and the crops grow wonderfully with the bare minimum of effort. You've built a sturdy house and made it a home. You're very handy so you also built an inn, a saloon, and a craft shop where you sell the essentials and do some blacksmith work.

When people arrive, there is no doubt it was you that built this town and the day has finally come when you get your first visitor.

Ecstatic, you welcome this person with open arms and they soon make themselves welcome in the inn. Later that night another visitor arrives and your happiness shoots through the roof. You have built this town for others after all. You are the creator, but this was developed as a gift for others to make their own, get on their feet, and develop the skills they need in life.

16

The next morning you see the first citizen of your new town come out of the inn and you ask how their stay has been so far.

"Terrible!" Says citizen one. The bed was too hard, the latrine was too far away, and going to the bathroom in the middle of the night was too much effort. The water running over the rocks was too loud, disturbing my sleep." "When is breakfast? I want to eat right now!" Says citizen one.

Heartbroken, you explain there is no one to cook breakfast yet and they must hunt and cook for themselves.

"What good then is this place for?!" Screams citizen one as he storms off to get a rifle to go stir up some breakfast. Detracted, you sit back in your chair in disbelief. You thought you did a really great job with your little town. A few moments later citizen two comes walking out of the inn whistling with a little hop in his step. You ask how his stay was and you become rejuvenated by the answer.

"Amazing!" Says citizen two. The bed was so very comfortable. And it was such a lovely walk to the latrine in the middle of the night. The insects serenaded me and the stars were amazing to gaze at! The water running over the rocks helped relax the stress of the day and I slept like a dream! Thank you for building such a wonderful place for people to live.

Now, as the creator of this town, which citizen would you more like to hang out with? Support if they need it? Get a beer maybe, if they ask? You already know where I'm going with this.

This first and most important rule for accessing The Everspace is realizing life is all about perspective and there is no room for negativity.

Jean-Paul Sartre said, "Hell is other people." I'm intent to prove this statement wrong by the end of this book. Notice I said prove the statement wrong, not the person. If I were arguing with Mr. Sartre I'd say, "Hell is your perspective of other people." This means to say if you view other people as Hell, it will be Hell for you. If you recognize and appreciate the humanity in every person and refuse to judge whether someone is good or bad, then hell will not develop.

Without other people, none of us would be where we are at today. People claim to be self-made, however it was the community of two people that initially made said person. If they are self-made then I assume they built the hospital they were born in, invented the medicine that kept them alive at birth, taught themselves to speak, walk and ride a bike. They sewed all their own clothes and built the house they lived in (I enjoy listening to wealthy people say, "We're building a house on such and such road." I say you're not building a house, you're having it "built"). I'd ask this so-called self-made person how many cars they built from scratch, and if they don't have a car, how many trains, and busses they made, and ask about how many roads they paved or sidewalks they cemented from concrete if they like to walk.

Like I said, without other people, everything we have, everything we enjoy in life today would cease to exist. This is where most of you put the book down and say, "O.K. I get your drift!" This is where I say, "It's all about perspective, my friend."

What Is It, Really?

Perspective. Per-spec-tive. Per-spek-tiv. Noun. It sounds provocative, but what does it really mean? The dictionary states it in this way: the state of one's ideas, the facts known to one, etc., in having a meaningful interrelationship. Meaning. People won't be compelled to change without it. After all, who wants to do something, for nothing? The very fact that you are reading this book shows that you do want to make a change in your life, but may not have the tools to build the future you want. Let's go back to perspective for a minute.

Perspective is the one word in this book that once firmly grasped, will render all other words in this book useless. You will, in a sense, realize that it is ALL about perspective. When we talk about perspective we are talking about an idea, yes, but more accurately we are talking about a programmed response in your brain that in any crisis will pull the positive information to the forefront of your thinking. Wrecked your car? At least no one was harmed. Failed a test? By default, I will do better on the next one. Failed again? Third time is a charm, and so on. The state of our thinking, or rather the state of our mind, is what is going to dictate our mood for the most part on a day-to-day basis. The fact of the matter remains that if we wake up and don't like the shirt we have on, or if our pants are too tight and uncomfortable, we either buy another pair or reach in the closet for something else to wear. We would never go to school not looking the way we want to, yet for some reason we wake up with the same negative thoughts every day and refuse to change. Changing clothes takes time and money, yet to change the way we think costs us nothing at all. The issue becomes habit and resistance. Like we see in the movie Room (1), a young boy born in captivity knows nothing but the contents of that little shed. He thinks that is freedom, his mother knows different and that is cause for sadness. When the mother finally devises a way for them to escape, the boy becomes confused and resists.

Examples of perspective are everywhere whether you realize it or not. Remember Tom Hanks at the end of Cast Away (2)? He just spent an inhumane amount of time alone on an island and had to fish and feed himself enduring many hardships along the way. When he is rescued, his friends throw a party for him and after everyone leaves, he is in the room, alone, next to a table of food. He picks up a crab leg and looks at it in disgust. It was at that moment that he realized how good we have it. For months he had to hunt and catch his own food. Now it's waiting for him at a moment's notice. Talk about appreciation.

The fact that we can go to the store and everything from cookies to fruit to steak and seafood is sitting right there for us is a blessing. In fact, ask anyone who was lost at sea, or hiking and ran out of food if they cherish every meal thereafter. The old saying, "You never know what you have till it's gone" rings very true here.

I believe that every person has the ability to change their perspective in their life, regardless of your current life situation. All you have to do is look at WHAT you have, and not at what you DON'T have. Herein lies the struggle. Growing up in America, you are taught from a very young age that you are entitled to more of everything. Don't like your job? Get a new one! Not making enough money? Ask for a raise, or get a job with a bigger salary! Then get a bigger house or more expensive car! Get the prettiest girl you can find! This is the American Dream. Sure, it's great to have nice things, but not having them should never be a cause for unhappiness!

The way we change the way we think about this is to stop comparing everything we have to what everyone else has. When we compare, we judge, and in turn create our own unhappiness. That's right. Read it again. YOU and you alone create your OWN unhappiness just by the way you are thinking. Like we say, it's all about perspective.

The main problem is we live in a society where you can turn on Channel 7 and see how much money someone else has, or open up Instagram on your phone and see where someone else went on vacation and become jealous, or envious, or "want" something other than what we have right now.

Judging is a crippler when it comes to changing the way you think, and was a real struggle for me over the years. But after learning a few tricks, my chronic judgments about people, or situations have greatly diminished over the years.

Judging People

Back in 2012, I developed a school mentorship program for a non-profit I used to work for called The Bess Route Foundation. At the beginning of our school presentation, I appear on stage in a costume of my choice purely to provoke a reaction from the crowd and instantly produce judgment. How often do we look at others and notice every negative thing about them before we can pick up one positive? I would never wear that shirt. Those shorts are terrible. Those are the worst earrings I've ever seen. That purse doesn't match those shoes. The list goes on and on and could fill up volumes of books if we so choose. When you judge someone immediately, you deny yourself the ability to ever truly meet that other person. You limit the things you can talk about by generating these negative thoughts. Having a positive perspective when meeting people opens up the door for conversation. All you have to do is focus on your similarities at the most basic human level and keep your heart open. The fact that you have the right to happiness, want to avoid suffering at all costs, are both part of a family, and live in the same part of the United States are a good start. We will get more into this in chapter 6, but I wanted to touch on it for a moment here. In the school presentation, I talk about seeing my client and former NFL wide receiver Davone Bess for the first time, and ask the audience where I would be, or what I would be doing today if I judged him on all of our differences rather than our similarities. He was an African American from East Oakland who just got out of jail, and I was a white guy from Buffalo, New York.

As our relationship developed, our similarities became more evident. We both had a passion for training, he wanted to be a better player, and I wanted to be a better coach. We ate the same food most of the time and each listed Michael Jordan as our favorite athlete. Judgment limits the amount of life situations you want to share with someone else by assuming they won't understand. If you stop judging, your relationships will grow, and you will increase your opportunities to meet people.

You never know who is going to be successful one day. I saw a story on the news about the most successful car salesman in the nation. His secret was that he treated every person the same no matter how they looked. In fact, he said if a 10-year-old boy came in he would treat him the same as everyone else and try to sell him a car too!

We need to stop judging people based off how they look; your success in life depends on it. I love following James Altucher's advice he gives in his book Choose Yourself (3)! James says that whenever he finds himself judging people, he adds a question mark at the end of a sentence and turns the statement into a question. I laughed when I first read about it, but it really works when you put it into practice. Here are the same statements I made earlier, but here I turn them into questions:
I would never wear that shirt?
Those shorts are terrible?
Those are the worst earrings I've ever seen?
That purse doesn't match those shoes?
I'm Ron Burgandy?
OK, OK, that last one was an Anchorman (4) plug but you get the picture!

When you question judgment, a certain innocence remains and relaxes you from that judgment, whereas statements regard something as definite. You start to think you are right. This has helped me tremendously ever since I read about it, and I'm confident it will help you too.

Judging Situations

William Shakespeare said, "Nothing is either bad, nor good, but thinking makes it so." This goes back to what I said earlier about you being the cause of your own

23

happiness. Thinking positive isn't a mindset it's a lifestyle. You don't think positive 50% of the time, and whatever else the remaining 50. You should be looking at the positive aspects of any situation whether society thinks it is good or bad. Have you ever been around the co-worker that is always happy no matter what? They are always smiling and laughing and you don't know why? Nothing seems to bother them and sometimes that bothers you. What these people practice every day is what can be characterized as flexible thinking.

Flexible thinking is a concept created to help people help themselves. Whether you realize it or not, you practice flexible thinking every day. Let me explain.
What happens when you are walking in the woods and come across a huge boulder in your way? Do you turn around and go home and say, "Guess we can't hike today!"? No, you simply climb over it, or find a way around and continue hiking.

Life is going to place boulders in front of you while you're trying to advance, and for some reason people just want to pack up and call it quits. For instance, when my client Davone went to jail and lost his scholarship, he wrote four different plans in his journal about what he was going to do when he got out. This is an example of flexible thinking.

If Path A is blocked, I resort to Path B. If I get stopped at B, do I turn around and go home? No! I have a Plan C. Look back on your life when you quit something. Were there other outlets? I know hindsight is 20/20, but often times we give up just too darn easy. The Everspace will not come to quitters! The Universe will simply bypass you with what it wants manifested and move on to someone

24

else. We need to go into every situation with as many backup plans as possible if we truly want to be creative. Let's look at this example:

Student A wants to make the Varsity basketball team as a freshman. If he makes it, great, but if not, what should he/she do?

Plan A - Try out for the JV team.
Plan B – If I don't make the JV team, then I'll try out for the freshman team.
Plan C – If I don't make the freshman team, I'll ask the coach if I can at least practice with the team in order to get better.
Plan D – If he doesn't let me practice, I'll watch as many practices as I can to familiarize myself with the offense, then go and practice on my own every day.
Plan E – I can play against bigger stronger kids at the playground to make me better so that way when I play against kids my own age it will be easier.

The list can go on and on as long as your planning is flexible and keeps to the same end result – playing basketball on one of those three teams.

The key to success is writing things down. Don't believe me? A study was made of alumni 10 years out of Harvard to find out how many were achieving their goals. An astounding 83% had no goals at all. Fourteen percent had goals, but they were not written down. Those people made more than three times what the people with no goals made. However, the three percent that had written goals were earning 3 times that of the people who had goals, and a whopping 10 times that of those that had no goals (5). Let me make that a little clearer.

Let's say people with no goals are making a minimum wage of seven dollars an hour, this is what the pay scale would look like:

No goals - $7 an hour

Goals - $21 an hour

Written down goals - $63 to $70 an hour!!!!!!!

I had a goal written down to make at least $1000 a week back when I graduated with my master's degree from The University of Hawaii. It was six months later that a job fell into my lap where I was making over $1500 a week and it wasn't even in the profession of my degree! Think positive, think flexible, and write down your goals. I know you're thinking this is hocus pocus, but here's the science behind what I'm talking about.

The Science to Thinking Positive

Ever since the field of Psychology was developed, doctors have been studying primarily negative emotions, or what provokes negative emotions, in hopes to find out what's wrong with society and correct some of its problems. Eight years ago, there was a shift in consciousness and The Journal of Personality and Social Psychology (6) was developed in order to study happiness. Yes, that's right, people get paid to create studies and find out why or how we can become happier (bless their souls). Their findings have been nothing short of astounding.

* In a study at the University of Wisconsin, women were shown pictures of people that were burned or disfigured

and were asked to write about it. The exercise resulted in an increased amount of satisfaction with their life.

* In another experiment at The State University of New York at Buffalo, subjects were asked to complete the sentence "I'm glad I'm not a..." After five repetitions of this exercise, subjects felt a distinct elevation in their feelings of life satisfaction. Another group of students was asked to complete the sentence "I wish I were a..." This time the experiment left the subjects feeling more dissatisfied with their life.

* Studies have shown that even purely academic education is directly linked to a happier life. Surveys found that higher levels of education have a positive correlation with better health and a longer life, and even protect an individual from depression.

* A study at Emory University showed that people who thought human beings were generally evil were significantly less happy than people who believed human beings were generally good.

* Scientists have found that if negative emotions are left unchecked, they will carry over to other situations that have absolutely nothing to do with the original situation that triggered the emotion.

* Dr. Barbara Fredrickson conducted many experiments showing how thinking positively, and positive emotions, actually act as antidotes to other surrounding negative emotions. She also proved that positive emotions lead to broader thinking, and broader thinking leads to positive emotions! In other words, positive thinking helps you come up with more successful ideas and vice versa!

* Dr. Martin Seligman found that when pessimists explain a bad situation, they attribute it to causes or negative conditions that will persist for a long time, and will affect other areas of their life, undermining everything they do. Optimists on the other hand, see things as temporary. For instance: Pessimist boy flunks a test and thinks, "I'll probably end up failing this test and flunk out of school!" Whereas optimist girl would say, "I've failed this exam, but I won't fail others and I'll just do better next time"

* John Cassel did a study that showed we react to stress in the direct way that we perceive it. If we don't perceive an event as being that stressful, our chances of being negatively impacted are not as great. In other words, life is all about perspective!

* Last but not least, experiments showing that people who had positive emotions could better detect the link between "elevator" and "Camel." They are both modes of transportation! How many of you got that one!!!!!!

I Love It When You Complain, Said the Brain

I once read an article written by Jessica Stillman for Inc.com entitled, "Complaining is Terrible for You, According to Science" that was compelling to say the least. From the first few sentences, she compares complaining to emotional farting in a closed area. Yes, you read that right, emotional farting.

Science has come to realize that when we formulate a thought, our brain sends a chemical across to the proper synapse over an empty space we call a synaptic cleft. This signal builds a bridge, which carries the information you are thinking.

The more this thought occurs, the brain actually starts to bring the synapses closer together to make the signal fire faster and be easier to carry. If this thought is negative, it not only makes more negative thoughts formulate, but also increases the chances of random negative thoughts occurring throughout the day. What's scary is that you can be judging a situation, and even if you are trying to see the positive side of it, if the negative thought synapses are closer together, a negative thought will arise and make it harder for us to think positive, let alone act in a positive manner.

Stillman goes on to say that our brain also learns on its own. If we hang out with negative people, our brain actually "tries out" those negative emotions, even if for a quick second. This is called empathy, and it can happen without you even knowing. I once read a quote a long time ago from Jim Rohn that said, "You are the average of the five people you spend the most time with." Basically, if you hang around with friends that love to bitch, moan, and complain all of the time; you will become a negative ball of energy. Negativity closes you off to The Everspace!

According to Stillman again, here are 5 things we can do to deflect people's negativity:

1. Dress Happy – Wear a pair of socks or loud tie that makes people laugh or smile.
2. Come Prepared – Be ready for that negative friend with positive solutions.
3. Try Radical Empathy – Understand their position, then be happy it isn't you thinking, or acting that way.
4. De-Stress Your Body Constantly – Get enough sleep,

eat well, and workout to channel negativity or stop it in its tracks.

5. Train Them With Your Attention – Elaborate on positive comments, and neutralize negative ones with phrases like "OK," or "I See."

The stress of negativity is terrible for your body. Next time you're venting to a friend or colleague, stop for a moment and focus on your heart rate, look at your reflection, and listen to your breathing. All of those will be in distress. Our emotional coherence is taking a dive and we will alter our ability to make solid decisions. This is where I would like to introduce HeartMath to you.

HeartMath

"Since emotional processing works faster than the mind, it takes a power stronger than the mind to bend perception, override emotional circuitry, and provide us with intuitive feeling instead. It takes the power of the heart."
-Doc Childre, Founder, Institute of HeartMath

The institute of HeartMath in California has been doing some compelling research for the past 20 years that really solidifies our thoughts on perspective and why it is so important to maintain a positive attitude and lead a positive lifestyle.

For years, we as human beings had only faith and belief to go on. Science, and the invention of technology have given us meaning as to why things should be done a certain way, and proof as to what works and what does not work. In the 1500's, the scientist Galileo proved that

30

we live in a Sun-centered solar system, not an Earth-centered solar system as we believed since probably the 4th century. In 1792, Christopher Columbus proved that the Earth was not flat, even though that was what scholars and philosophers previously said.

Science has put men on the Moon, and according to the Human Genome Project's report in the year 2000, that race is a myth, yet we still believe in race to this day. Science has changed the way we have viewed the world, and the work of HeartMath is no different. The problem as we see with race, is that old habits die hard with us human beings, and because of this fact, most people may be ready to dismiss their findings as pure rubbish. Let's see if we can change your mind.

HeartMath's belief through their research is that the brain does not control the heart; it is actually the other way around. When the heart beats and the valves open, there is a momentary pause before it beats again. HeartMath wanted to study what was going on during that second or so and became amazed by their findings.

It turns out that during the pause between heartbeats, the heart is sending an amazing amount of information to the brain about every structure of the body, most specifically the nervous system that can affect our intelligence and awareness. It does this through a bundle of 40,000 neurons called sensory neurites, which can detect circulating hormones and then send that information to the brain through afferent (flowing to the brain) nerve structures like the Vagus nerve.

They are finding also that the heart sends way more information to the brain than the other way around. So we

31

are presented with an alarming scientific realization here. If we pay close attention though, we shouldn't be that surprised. For centuries, religious paintings and sculptures have been depicting the heart as the center of the human body, whereas there are virtually no paintings or sculptures depicting an exposed brain.

Did we know this all along? Is this just another DUH moment that future human beings may look back on 100 years from now and laugh as we laugh at the thought of the world being flat, or the Earth being the center of the Universe? It certainly seems a possibility.

Who cares, Chris? Who cares that the heart controls the brain? After all this isn't a Biology textbook. The reason is simple. Positive and negative have a profound influence on the type of information the heart sends to the brain. What the pioneers at HeartMath are finding out is that negative emotions actually block the heart-brain connection from functioning optimally, and more specifically that negative emotions inhibit our ability to think properly.

That's right, your anger or negative thoughts and viewpoints that creep into your head day in and day out can actually deter proper brain activity, thus decreasing your success in school, the workplace, thought-provoking life situations, and ultimately access to The Everspace. Let's look at some of the experiments they have done and see what we can conclude:

* Concentrations of Oxytocin, the "love" hormone is as high in the heart as they are in the brain.

* Once an emotion is experienced, it becomes a powerful

32

motivator of future behaviors. The reaction almost becomes programmed and will affect moment-to-moment action as well as long-term action.

* People growing up experiencing anger or fear regularly get trapped in a repetitive emotional pattern and their hormonal and neural systems develop the same patterns as well.

* Chronic, unmanaged emotional stress is as much as six times more predictive of cancer and heart disease than cigarette smoking, cholesterol level or blood pressure, and is also more responsive to intervention.

* The autonomic nervous system, which regulates things like breathing, heart rate, and hormone function, is affected by our emotions. Negative emotions disrupt the balance, and positive emotions align the function of the heart, brain and lungs, causing them to operate more efficiently.

Psychophysiological Coherence

The hippies had it right back in the 70's, and John Lennon of The Beatles was spot on when he said, "All you need is love." When you look at the hustle and bustle in the world today, you can't help but start to feel anxiety. There is noise everywhere. Cars, busses, horns, music, bells, alarms, voices over intercoms. From the minute we wake up till the moment we go to bed there is always noise. The underlying issue with this is that all this noise causes stress, regardless if you know it or not. Stress causes an increase in the amount of a hormone called cortisol in your body. Cortisol is an adrenal hormone that when elevated

33

regularly, can have detrimental effects on the basic functioning of the human body. Worst of all is that it promotes fat storage. As human beings evolved, they lived in almost complete silence for 3 million years, only hearing the wind, rain, and sounds of their own voices. They operated more on intuition, went to sleep shortly after the sun went down, and woke up when the sun arose the next day.

As humans, this was our biorhythm so to say. Now we have night shifts, shades, and alarms that allow us to sleep at any point of the day. We have bills, deadlines, and alimony to worry about. The lack of sleep people function on day to day has prompted a huge increase in the amount of sugary, caffeinated beverages companies make. As a result, we become dependent on an unnatural source of energy that negatively affects our body and our wallet. The research being done at HeartMath on an idea called psychophysiological coherence shows what a detriment stress and anger can be on the inside functioning of the human body.

Psychophysiological coherence is the scientific term for saying the heart, brain, and lungs are electrically aligned. When these organs align, we create balance, and only a balanced being can enter The Everspace.

For their first experiment, the researchers at HeartMath hooked up electrodes and monitored a person's heart rate variability, pulse rate transit time, and respiration, and showed that while the person was tense or angry, all three of those readings would be erratic and out of sync. However, when the subjects focused on a deep appreciation of love for themselves and coupled that with positive thinking, all three of those variables aligned, and the heart, pulse rate, and lungs were all firing on virtually the same frequency. When this occurred, there was an overall better feeling of well-being in the subjects and there was no doubt their body was running more efficiently.

The technique is called a heart lock-in and it's actually pretty simple to do. All you have to do is focus intensely on the center of your chest with as much love and appreciation as you can muster.

Heart Mathematicians have done clinical trials, as well as real-life trials with businessmen and women as well as police officers, (who probably have one of the most stressful careers there is) and achieved great success with all of them. They could all solve problems faster, and carried less stress after the workday was done. Who doesn't want that?

The findings don't stop there though. HeartMath has found that there is an actual measurable magnetic field that extends approximately 15 feet in diameter around each person's body. This electromagnetic field can actually generate information that can be sensed by others. This is dictated by the strength of the signal.

Depending on how close you are, your heartbeat signal can actually be registered by another person's brainwaves. If you are holding hands, and one person has a coherent heart-brain signal, that signal will actually be matched by the other person's brainwave.

Ever have the touch of someone else instantly calm you? Have you ever been really upset and then instantly better when a friend appeared? This may explain how we sometimes finish the sentences of our friends, or loved ones; our brains literally speak to each other through this heart field!

If you talk to the right people who had the chance to meet or make music with Bob Marley, they all say the same thing; you could "feel" his presence as he walked in the room. You could sense there was something different about him and people gravitated towards him and didn't know why.

Looking back with this information, the answer is readily available if you want to believe it. After all, his music was about love! Love and positivity! Nobody will deny that Bob could access The Everspace. His creative ability was unmatched for his age and he was a musical pioneer. We can remain a society that believes in being tough, or hardened, closing our hearts off to life and the situations it presents us to grow which will increase our stress and the stress of those around us. Or we can become loving, positive beings that actually will increase our own health and that of those around us. There is no doubt anymore that love and positivity are the way to a better life, and HeartMath is proving that.

There are words of wisdom all around us, but no one seems to listen. We may hear the beat and bob our head, but the message is in the words. We will learn more about Drake and his message later on in chapter 5, but for now we must realize it is all about perspective; that life will always be about how you view it and what you believe, and that is why positivity is the first point we want to make. After you instill a culture of positivity in yourself and those who are close to you, everything else will be easy.

Concluding Thoughts on Perspective

Scientists have confirmed that 99% of our thinking is repetitive. Erase the negative story of "me" you dwell on every day and you will open the gates for productive, creative thought patterns. Thinking positive, even in tough situations, will create space for your subconscious mind to kick into gear.

I mean seriously, think of all the negative bullshit you convince yourself of every day and think about where you would be if you replaced all of that with constructive, positive thinking!

Erase all of the negative aspects of your life, the people that allegedly hurt you, or maybe you don't like where you live. Those negative thoughts are not who you really are! They are there as a distraction. As humans, we have the ability to make real what we tend to believe. More often than not, we tend to distort our sense of reality in order to feed and give credibility to how we feel at the present moment.

Wouldn't you like all of those repetitive thoughts to be happy, productive thoughts? Happy thoughts free your mind and help you to be more creative in a positive way. Creating fearful thoughts, or projections of the future, disrupt the flow of the natural universe and create tension for us. Why? Because the future does not exist yet and therefore life has not given you the resources to deal with it so the only place for happiness is creating it now! Misery loves company, but it has to go out and search for other miserable people. Positivity on the other hand is contagious! All we have to do is think and act positive in any situation and anyone around us will eventually

37

gravitate to and agree with our point of view, expanding our options! Take the positive route in life and the possibilities will be endless.

People wake up every day and complain about the weather, or what they have to do that day. They don't like their car so they go to the car dealer and buy a new one. If you don't like your shirt, or the shoes you have, you can change them by buying new ones. If we don't like a TV show or radio station, we will be very quick to turn it off, or find something we like. The fact remains, however, that most of us wake up every day thinking negative thoughts like citizen one in the story at the beginning of this chapter. Adults may wake up and say, "I can't face this day, and I wish it were over already." Every day is another chance to learn something new and grow. Why would the Universe or the Divine allow you to enter an infinite space where you can do anything you want if it knows you don't want to grow?

Nothing in life does this. No animal, tree, flower, fish, or reptile wakes up and says, "I can't face another day." Stop judging and start turning your statements into questions. The harsh reality is that if we want to change something in our life as I mentioned earlier, like a car or new clothes, this usually costs money. However, there is no charge for changing the way you think about life or your current situation.

Changing your mind is free! I know what some of you are thinking right now, "Those trees and animals don't have any problems." Like we said earlier, there are no problems, only situations. We create problems by judging, by labeling them as such, and science proves that once we label something as negative, we destroy the heart-

38

mind balance and prohibit our ability to think properly. If we look at the reality of it, an animal or a flower doesn't know what a problem is; it simply sees the current situation as living life, then takes the appropriate action. You never knew what a problem was till someone explained what one was and then you bought into it! Yes, yes, my phone battery died and I'm at the school dance with no way to update my Facebook status. This is a serious problem!

No judgment.

No fear.

This is what philosophers may call tranquility. Stay positive, work with the negatives, and the picture of life changes to one of hope rather than despair, and The Everspace becomes clearer.

Your Key to Accessing The Everspace:

Gratitude VS. Thanks

Giving thanks to someone is not the same as gratitude. Thankfulness comes from the psyche, and is a thought form. Gratitude comes from the soul and is thus a connection to the divine. As far as the divine is concerned, you can fake being thankful as much as you want to another human being, but you can never fake gratitude because it is tied to your genuine self.

Gratitude originates deep within you. If someone opens your car door, you simply reply thank you, and go about your day. However, if someone saves your friend's life, you aren't just thankful for them, it goes deeper than that. This feeling is gratitude. Recognize the difference between the two, and practice more gratitude in your daily life.

Uncomfortability Challenge

Give up what I call "Crap Emotions." Crap emotions are what I consider to be any emotion that does not get you to where you want to go in your life. These can be, but are not limited to:

* Negativity
* Sadness
* Self-loathing
* Self-pity
* Ill-will
* Anger
* Righteous anger
* Jealousy
* Envy
* Fear
* Sorrow
* Grief
* Emptiness
* Frustration
* Guilt
* Depression
* Doubt
* Shame
* Revenge

You cannot access The Everspace with these emotions in your heart or mind. Give them up! How do you give them up? When you start feeling these emotions, simply tell yourself you're not interested in feeling that right now. Recognize those feelings don't serve you. If that doesn't work, simply stop acknowledging them, or have a song ready that makes you happy and play it every time these emotions creep in.

Now I'm not saying you should walk around emotionless, it's the carrying of these emotions that are detrimental. Start off feeling them for a day, then a couple of hours, then a couple of minutes, and then you can feel them pass right through you. Getting rid of these emotions changes your life in unimaginable ways!

Exercises

Finish this sentence ten times, with ten different hypothetical results:

I'm glad that.........

1.

2.

3.

4.

5.

6.

7.

8.

9.

10.

List three positive things that can come from the following scenarios:
Your phone broke in the middle of the day and you can't get a replacement till the next day.

1.

2.

3.

The girl or guy you want to ask out already has a significant other.

1.

2.

3.

Your boss gave someone else the promotion instead of you.

1.

2.

3.

Your car broke down.

1.

2.

3.

Finally, one last question to ask yourself:
Do you feel you can access something in a timeless
realm while still living under the constraints of time?

References:

1. Abrahamson, L. (Director). (n.d.) Room [Video file].
Retrieved from http://roomthemovie.com/
2. Zemeckis, R. (Director). (n.d.). Cast away [Video file].
3. Altucher, J. (2013). Choose Yourself: Be happy, make
millions, live the dream. Lioncrest Publishing.
4. McKay, A. (Director), McKay, A., & Ferrell, W. (Writers),
& Apatow, J. (Producer). (n.d.). Anchorman: The legend of
Ron Burgandy [Video file].
5. Kublin, M.W., Mayer-Rodriguez, J. 12 Steps for
Courageous Leadership: Start Your Journey Now!
AuthorHouse, April 26, 2011.
6. Personality and Social Psychology. (n.d.). The Oxford
Handbook of Personality and Social Psychology.
Doi:10.1093/oxfordhb/9780195398991.013.0001

EverLesson 2: Everything Happens for a Reason

"We are caught in an inescapable web of mutuality, tied in a single garment of destiny. Whatever affects one directly, affects all indirectly. That is the way the world is made."

-Dr. Martin Luther King Jr.

"There are moments when troubles enter our lives and we can do nothing to avoid them. But they are there for a reason. Only when we have overcome them will we understand why they were there."

- Paulo Coelho, The Fifth Mountain

Steven R. Covey wrote probably one of the best books on personal development called The Seven Habits of Highly Effective People (1). In the first few pages of the book he presents us with this picture:

Depending on your psyche, you will either see an old lady, or a young lady. Which one did you see? Did you see the young lady with her head turned away from you or did you see the old lady with her chin tucked to her chest? Covey does this to illustrate a point. Two people can look at the same thing and see something totally different. "It's not logical, it's psychological." He says.

There are a thousand ways that things can work out in any aspect of your life and it's nobody's fault! The first key element to this lesson it to stop pointing fingers and blaming others. I encourage you to even stop blaming yourself. Guilt is a crap emotion! It leads down victim lane and that's not where The Everspace resides, which is why those that play the victim in life will never be where they want to be or do what they want to do.

There are many people who say believing that everything happens for a reason provides false hope when the system breaks down. What it really provides is neutrality and acceptance. When life is good, we're happy, yet when something we consider to be bad happens, we look for the first person we can put blame on and this distracts us from the lesson life is trying to teach.

One of the traps many fall into is righteous anger as well. I don't care if the devil himself shows up at your doorstep and tells you how right you are; don't believe it! Give it up. Say softly in your mind that this event is happening for a reason and meditate or reflect on that reason. Life will show you when you look, but if you're not searching, life isn't telling.

Most people think that our life should look like an ascending line on a graph. The older we get, the wiser we get, the less problems we have and so on. This is completely untrue, and the wrong way to look at what I am saying. The very fact that we ascend, or climb UP the ladders in life, implies that at one point we were LOWER than we are right now. Up and down are both parts of the same whole.

Many of the smartest and most successful people believe everything happens for a reason, and I feel they are correct. Having this belief gives your life purpose, and this is one of the key elements to accessing The Everspace.

46

You need to find out what your purpose is in life. When you believe everything happens for a reason, you blend the control of your life's happenings between you, AND the divine.

This is partly what the Bible means when it says God has given us freewill. We all serve a purpose; whether we are listening to what that purpose is depends on what we are about to learn.

The world is a crazy place. Don't believe me? Just turn on the news and watch the Trump/Clinton presidential debate, or read a book on any one of the 7 crusades. There are currently over 7 billion people on the planet and that number is only going to get bigger. The more people that inhabit planet Earth, the more pressure we will put on our ecosystem to produce food for us, produce clean water to drink, we will depend on the environment to decompose our garbage, dilute our pollution from cars and coal burning plants, and so on.

When the basic needs (food, clothing, shelter) become scarce in the world, what are we going to do? About one in every ten million living creatures on Earth is a human being, which makes us a biological miracle. We are a rarity in this world and yet we create most of the destruction in this world. Human behavior is downright puzzling sometimes.

To believe that we are all tied together in a single garment of destiny like Dr. King says is a very hard concept for some people to grasp. Ideas like fate are brought in to play, and some people dismiss the concept because they want to think they have more control in their life. When we think we are in control, we are really flowing with what is, and being present. When we feel we are losing control, we are fighting life and resisting what is, essentially missing our appointment with the here and now.

In the documentary, God Grew Tired of Us (2), a Sudanese refugee named John who walked 1,000 miles to a safe camp in Kakuma after a civil war broke out said, "I believe everyone has a talent. God made me very tall, and he did not make me tall for nothing. So it is my duty to find out what my purpose is for being tall. I must keep searching for my meaning in life. This is my duty."

Hopefully this chapter will persuade you to not be one of those people that feel life has no meaning, or that you are worthless, because you are not. Everyone has a function in society, and everyone has a purpose. It is up to us to find out what it is. Pay attention to life and it will show you. You can call it fate or destiny or whatever you want, but I have been paying attention to the signs for years now. Don't get me wrong; this is not some type of dogma or religion. All I am asking is that when you think back on what happened in your life, are there any signs as to why they happened? One of the things that makes life confusing is when people consider life to be too random. They consider themselves to be "unlucky" or accept the fact that "life hates me" or one of my personal favorites, "the whole world is against me."

I used to convince myself of these things. I used to think I could create my own destiny and when things didn't go my way I would be confused, mad even. This is not the case. Life, Infinite Intelligence, The Divine, whatever you want to call it, was always teaching me a very valuable life lesson, and if I was not being present, it would just float on by. Life it seems, very rarely gives you second chances.

The Field

"As you look upon creation, which appears so solid and real, remember to always think of it as the thought of God frozen into physical forms. You can condition your mind to this realization in little ways each day. Whenever you see a beautiful sunset, think to yourself: It is God's painting on the sky"

-Paramahansa Yogananda

When you look at the world, what do you see? What do you feel? What do you hear? What do you taste? What do you smell? All of these questions relate to what is called our sense perceptions. All living things perceive the world in a different way, through different senses. Humans are big on seeing things as the old saying goes, "seeing is believing." If you were to talk to a dog, the dog would probably say, "Seeing is ok, but for me smelling is believing." Talk to a bat and the bat is going to say, "I can't smell good, and I definitely can't see, so to me, hearing is believing." Senses are a relationship; they help us traverse through what we call reality.

Reality

What is real this day and age? Real is what you perceive. According to Newtonian physics, our world is very mechanistic. If you do this, such and such will happen. It's how we view the body as well. Cells divide according to encoded DNA information, chemicals and hormones fire at alarming rates (every cell undergoes 100,000 chemical reactions per second (3)) that produce signals that go to the brain, where the brain interprets the data and sends it

49

back throughout the body. If one function stops working, the machine is broken, signals get lost and your body is said not to be "working" properly. The problem with the mechanistic view is that it does not apply very well to living things as we are finding out. Well, it does and it doesn't. If I take my computer apart and I know everything about computers and put it back together, it should work the same as before. If I dissect my cat, and take out every organ, and I'm the best surgeon in the world, even if I put everything back together, my cat will most likely not "work" anymore (4). Where it gets a little weird is an experiment done on rats. In 1946, Karl Lashley wanted to find out what part of the brain was responsible for memory, so he trained rats to jump off a platform where there would be a reward for food. The rats that did not do it properly were met with a short fall into a pond of water. After the rats were trained, he then crudely operated on the rats, burning parts of their brain with his wife's curling iron, hoping to hit the spot responsible for memory. To his disillusionment, after the rats recovered, they still remembered exactly what they were taught. Some rats would stagger along and be physically impaired, but their memory was not affected.

Lashley started to think. What if cognition or memory did not reside in the brain? What if the brain was a medium to recall events, and not an actual storage facility for memory? Enter The Field.

There's a theory in quantum physics that goes something like this: an object such as an atom exists in all states you can imagine until it is observed. When this atom is being looked at, it actually "freezes" as the observer does the observing, and when he or she is done observing, the atom then disappears. It exists when looking at it, but then ceases to exist, or changes when you stop looking at it. Confusing? Yes. That's because the only thing that is certain in quantum physics is that nothing is for certain. As early as Einstein, physicists were playing with the idea of a field of energy that cannot be seen or felt, yet only accessed through intense awareness. Scientists have since termed this energy source the Zero Point Field. Einstein is recorded to have said many times, "The Field is the only thing that is real." Since Einstein was kind of a smart guy, we'll trust him for a second.

The zero-point field was once thought of to be a place where nothing existed. And since nothing existed, then nothing could be measured. One day, scientists started noticing activity in the field, and soon enough they started to devise ways to measure the energy in the field and started to theorize and experiment as only scientists do. What they were finding was amazing, baffling, and downright unacceptable sometimes.

Their experiment pointed to energy in the field that operates on wavelengths that in turn causes protons and electrons to vibrate. This vibration causes a ripple effect moving from atom to atom. Old Newtonian physics stated there were different states of energy. Through the field, scientists were finding that matter was not a fundamental property of physics. They were showing that Einstein's famous equation $E=MC2$ was a recipe for the amount of energy needed for the appearance of mass, or that there are not two fundamental properties of physics, one material and one immaterial; in fact, the only property to physics was energy. No matter what we see in this world, be it planes to buildings to sticks and stones, it's all just a collection of electric charges that the field brings into a state of coherence for our senses to witness. Think of

Neo in The Matrix (5). When he dies and comes back to life in the first movie, he sees people, walls, floors – everything is just number coded differently to make them what they are. There's no identification with solid objects, just code. Still following me?

We heard about coherence in HeartMath, showing that if you affect the main control system of the body, in this case the heart, you can force not only your body to work more efficiently, but if in close contact, or holding hands with another individual, you can influence their system to run more efficiently as well. The field does this to all things in nature. Scientists show you just have to be aware, or "in tune" with the idea and you can actually start to control aspects of your life you once felt were out of your control. Vishen Lakhiani, owner of a personal growth platform called Mindvalley calls it "Bending Reality."

Realizing that things happen for a reason forces you to pay attention to the signs or signals that life or the field is trying to send to you. Believing things to be a coincidence, or saying that events occur due to fate is the first step to dismissing the "realness" of the field.
OK, so back to Karl Lashley and his rats. Lashley was formulating the idea that maybe memory did not reside in the brain; maybe it resided in The Field. How else can you explain that if you want to recall things that happened years ago, the memory is right there? You don't have to go sifting through years of memories to get the right one. The way theorists were figuring was that The Field is the only thing that contains everything from the past to the future, and when we needed a memory our brains would just pluck it from The Field as we subconsciously access any and all life occurrences. After all, it was just an exchange of energy, right?

If this is true, then the brain does not store memories; it receives them. Experiments have shown that salamanders can regenerate any part of their body as if some mysterious blueprint for it exists in their DNA. What if they can sense and understand The Field better than other living things? A sort of real-life Yoda whom this alleged force is the strongest with. People who lose a limb claim to have a "phantom limb" experience as to where they can feel cramps, or pain where the amputated limb used to be.

What if human beings could tap into the salamander's power of The Field? What if The Field is telling those amputees that the energy to regenerate their limb is right in front of their face if they would only pay close enough attention? It is often the cleverest solutions to any situation that reside out in the open as we search elsewhere.

Think about it, when you look at something like a ball in the grass, the perception of it is actually created in the retina and sent to the brain. But you don't reach into your retina to grab the ball; you reach down onto the ground where you perceive the ball to be. So, the world in a sense is just a virtual creation or 3-D environment, with a 4th dimension which psychics, clairvoyants, artists, and scientist are accessing regularly.

Are we really getting smarter as human beings evolve? Technology may be growing and becoming more convenient, yes, but are we as in synch with the world as we used to be, or even as in synch with the world as our dog or cat? We will get into more interesting research on that topic soon, but for now just ponder that question. When I think about this type of information, it reminds me of the song by Jack Johnson – Traffic in the Sky. He says, "Wisdom's all around, but no one seems to listen." Are we really that busy? Are we becoming more attuned to our phone updates or Facebook status and ignoring all the signs of life? Are we becoming mechanized human beings like in the movie Wall-E (6)? Are we going to be carted around by coasters that defy gravity, dispensing with the need for us to walk or exercise?

It seems the more we think, the more we get things to do stuff for us, and the result is paying more attention to screens than to trees. Soon we will be buying more batteries to power things that replace the need for real people. Jack continues in the song to say, "Puzzle pieces on the ground, but no one seems to be diggin'." What we truly need to be happy is already inside of us, but most are not paying attention to the signs of life so they end up confused, hurt, or angry.

Lynne McTaggart wrote "The Field" under what I can imagine to be great duress, because in a sense what she is offering is a replacement for God, and that doesn't sit too well with some people. What we need to do is go back to enjoying life, and not chasing or feverishly wanting material things. We need to tap back into nature because after all we are nature! It sounds silly, it sounds utopian, and I'm sure most of you are shaking your heads by now, but like they say in quantum physics, if you're not paying attention to it, then technically it doesn't exist.

The evidence in the field is overwhelming. Robert Janh created the Princeton Engineering Anomalies research (PEAR) program and did thousands upon thousands of studies with random event generators. People would come in hours at a time and watch a computer flip a coin on the screen randomly generating heads or tails. Jahn briefed his subjects and had some mentally influence the computer to generate more heads than tails, and had other subjects generate more tails than heads. In almost every case, what the subject mentally willed, the random event generator produced. What he noticed though was that you could not have a crazy, out-of-control mental vision; it had to be calm and relaxed in order to tap into The Field's energy.

Remember, it is all about coherence though. Often times you see people in the world who try to have the most control and power over everyone, whether it be in business, or relationships, but in actuality, they have the least amount of control over their own lives. Things need to flow, they need to resonate freely and have order in order for any good to come out of it. McTaggart States,

"PEAR studies may suggest that we can help create order in the world. When we wish for something or intend something, an act, which takes a great deal of unity and thought, our own coherence may be in a sense, infectious. On the most profound level, the PEAR studies suggest that reality is created by each of us only by our ATTENTION. At the lowest level of mind and matter, each of us creates the world. By the simple act of wishing calmly, we can create order. This is proof that when it comes down to it, life really is mind over matter. By the act of observation and intention, we have the ability to extend a kind of super-radiance into the world."

Why aren't more people talking about this? Why aren't more people practicing this? Why isn't this being taught in our schools? Why do we still feel the need to complain when it's a zero-sum game and gets us nowhere? Why do we still listen to people who complain? If our intentions can affect the world, or more interestingly affect the machines we use, is it any wonder that in a whole office of negative people, or constant tension-stress environments, things keep breaking down? From cars to copiers to computers, what if they broke because of our negativity toward them every day. It's actually not the machine that's broken, but our connection to it. That brings new meaning to everything happening for a reason.

We believe that these objects are inanimate, or not "alive," and that may be true, but there is a connection we need to be aware of. Treat that new iPhone disrespectfully and no wonder it stops working for you. Send negative texts all day and shout into it, and you'll be out $600 with very quickly. People say talk to your plants and they will be healthier. What if we have to start talking nicely to our electronics, or our cars in order for them to work properly? Would it be strange waking up to get the newspaper and your neighbor is whispering sweet nothings to his new BMW?

Plant cognition has been tested many times before and it has been shown that they do produce a measurable amount of stress. Hal Putoff sent a proposal to Cleve Backster, a New York polygraph expert, to test whether or not plants had any emotion. They hooked a plant up to electrodes used in a lie detector test and proceeded to burn a leaf of the plant. To Backster's surprise, the plant showed electrical activity equivalent to a human having his or her hand burnt.

What was more interesting was they burned the leaf of a plant that was not touching or associated with the first plant and it still registered stress as if it could feel the other plant's pain! Still don't believe there's a Zero Point Field yet? Still don't think everything is divinely orchestrated, that we're all connected, and everything happens for a reason? I trust this is just the tip of the iceberg, and as science evolves, so will their findings.

Creating Your Own Path

"Chance determines the cards you are dealt, but freedom lies in how you play them out."

-Unknown

Believing that everything in your life happens for a reason dismisses randomness in life. It should teach us to never take a smile, a glance, or a chance meeting for granted ever again. Believing everything happens for a reason gives meaning to the moments of our lives. We have happiness to erase the sadness, we get taught that suffering is grace, and pain tells us that our connection to life is fragile. How many of us are listening?

In the movie JOBS, Ashton Kutcher plays Steve Jobs, mastermind behind Apple Computer products. Many people will watch the movie and remark on how crazy or out of control Jobs' persona was. What people don't realize is that in order to create your own path in life you need to innovate, and innovation does not come with a set of instructions. Often times these people who are creating their own path in life are seen as mad, and it is somewhat true because at times, not even they know where they are going or what they are doing, but it is the consistency and persistence that brings their vision to fruition.

You get a sense in the movie that nothing was ever good enough for Jobs, and that's because he was a CREATOR. When you create, you want to perfect, and in order to perfect you need PERSISTENCE and a high attention to detail. When you are trying to create something, you are given the questions first then you have to go find the answers, yet we are all brought up in a school system where we are given the answers first, then given the questions. As Robert Kiyosaki says, "This makes great employees, but horrible bosses."

You cannot predict the future, but you can reflect positively on your past and try to connect the dots to find out why things happened the way they did in your life. It's kind of like detective work. Here is a great example from a speech Jobs gave in front of the graduating class at Stanford in 2005 (7):

"I dropped out of Reed College after 6 months or so, but then stayed around as a drop-in for 18 months before I really quit. So why did I drop out? It started before I was born. My biological mother was a young unwed graduate student and she decided to put me up for adoption. She felt very strongly that I should be adopted by college graduates so everything was all set for me to be adopted by a lawyer and his wife. Right after I was born, the lawyer and his wife decided that they really wanted a girl. So my parents, who were on a waiting list, got a call in the middle of the night and were asked if they wanted a boy. They said, "of course." My biological mother had found out later that my Mother had not graduated from college and my father had not graduated from high school. She refused to sign the final adoption papers. She only changed her mind a few days later when my parents promised her that I would go to college. Seventeen years

*later, I did go to college. But I chose a college that was so
expensive that it was eating up my parents' savings and I
just couldn't see the value in it. Looking back, it was one of
the best decisions I ever made. I could drop out of the
classes that didn't interest me, and drop in on the ones
that did. I slept in friends' rooms, and returned coke
bottles for the deposit and used that to get food."*

He goes on to say:

*"Reed College had one of the best calligraphy
programs in the nation. Everywhere on campus were
posters with beautiful typography and perfectly spaced
letters. The classes I sat in on about calligraphy
absolutely fascinated me. However, none of it had any
application to anything I was doing in my life at the time.
Later on however, when we were developing the first Mac,
everything came back to me and I applied what I learned
in to making the best computers available today. If I had
not dropped out of college, I would not have dropped in on
that class, and maybe none of the computers we use
today would have the beautiful typography they do. Of
course, it was impossible to connect the dots looking
forward in college, but now as I look backwards, it is very,
very clear. You have to trust that somehow the dots will
connect in your future. You have to trust in something.
Your gut, destiny, life, Karma, or whatever, because
believing that the dots connect down the road will give you
the confidence to follow your heart, even when it leads you
off the well-worn path, because that will make all the
difference."*

This is another huge lesson. When you listen to Mr. Jobs
speak, he uses words like passion, love, fascinate,
confidence. I also believe that when you put your all into

everything, you will eventually succeed. That is what most business owners and CEO's do. They take the less-beaten path and put their faith in hard work and dedication into EVERYTHING they do, not just into their business. When you start connecting the dots backwards, you start finding a greater meaning in life and you open yourself up more to others believing that they are not just chance meetings. You start seeing more of the good in people, thinking, "I'll give them a little more time to develop as a friend, girlfriend, business friend, etc. because they are in my life for a reason." It takes time for good things to develop, but the culture we grow up with in America that makes things so readily available makes us want things right now. Our young never develop patience.

We want to have someone tell us the reason why before we start believing in it. In his book The Alchemist (8), Paulo Coelho says:

"Before a dream is realized, the soul of the world tests everything that individual has learned along the way. It does this not because it is evil, but so that we can, in addition to realizing our dreams, master the lessons we learned as we moved towards that dream. That's the point at which most people give up. It's the point at which as we say in the language of the desert, one dies of thirst just as the palm trees have appeared on the horizon."

Don't die of thirst just when you see the palm trees on the horizon. Don't give up on your dreams. Because when you do, is most likely when that dream was finally going to happen.

Eckhart Tolle, one of the most forward thinkers on this topic has this to say,

"There are situations where all answers and explanations fail. Life does not make sense anymore. Or someone in distress comes to you for help, and you don't know what to do or say. When you fully accept that you don't know, you give up struggling to find answers with the limited thinking mind, and that is when a greater intelligence can operate through you. And even thought can then benefit from that, since the greater intelligence can flow into it and inspire it. Sometimes surrender means giving up trying to understand and becoming comfortable with not knowing."

The "greater intelligence" he is talking about is The Everspace. He then goes on to say,

"What seems to be in the way – IS the way. Use what goes wrong in your life to learn and experience from rather than try to shut it out and forget it. You're accepting life rather than denying it which is all you should ever do."
There were a couple important things that were said there. When it comes down to it, it's all about perspective. You can refuse to connect the dots, live life randomly and without meaning, constantly questioning your existence, or you can get over yourself for a minute. Sit down at a park and use your brain, instead of letting your brain use you. Tolle says things like "be comfortable not knowing," and, "what seems to be in the way, IS the way."

The problem with not knowing, or trying to connect the dots is that you may not find out why these events happened or why you met the people you did in your life for a week, a month, or several years. As long as you are patient, stay present, and reflect on the true nature of the signs, one day life will show you. Life will confirm how important of a role you play in the grand scheme of things;

all you have to do is be alert. Stop texting for a second.
Stop wishing you were someplace else (A key concept we
will help you understand better in Chapter 3) and realize
things are not happening to you, they are happening FOR
you.

Nothing Happens TO You

One of the most amazing shifts that occurred in my life
was when I took charge of how I felt about what had
happened in my life. I came to the realization as I was
connecting the dots backwards, that nothing ever happens
TO you (events, actions, emergencies, relationships, debt
etc.) but rather for you. Things happen in your life to force
you to grow.

When we look at life from the perspective that things
happen to us, we play the victim as well as give up control
of our own destiny. We play the passenger in life; make it
a passive process, rather than an active process.

In June of 2015 my wife left me. I didn't understand why, I
didn't see it coming, and I totally played the victim. I tried
to talk to friends and family members and get as much
sympathy as possible. I waited and waited for her to come
back and guess what?

My wife wasn't coming back to me.

Why is this happening to me? I thought. I'm a good
person. I have never cheated on her, I never lied to her,
and I never took this woman for granted. I'm not an
alcoholic and I never let a day or an opportunity go by
where I didn't tell her how much I loved her.

My first step to get out from under this cloud of darkness was to take a meditation vacation in Assisi, Italy. While many very good thoughts came to fruition during the 5-day meditation, the BIGGEST was this realization:

Things don't happen TO you, they happen FOR you.

What was happening for me? I was given the ability to compound time. Rather than sit around and watch reruns of the show Entourage (like I was doing before my vacation), I returned from Italy and started working feverishly on growing my business, finishing my nutrition book that I was dragging my feet on, and I purchased myself an apartment with the help of a consulting company through the use of credit cards. I was compounding time and getting stuff done that life wanted me to get done. The sense of accomplishment I have from completing my first book is worth 10 wives! I never thought it was possible, but it became possible as soon as I stopped playing the victim, and started learning from the situation.

I started to believe that my wife leaving me was a GOOD thing and took the opportunity of having more time to help myself, and help others as well. The result was nothing short of astounding.

What you'll notice is it was not just the realization I had, but the effort I put into the ACTION required to make these things happen. Let's find out what happens when there is no action behind realization.

A SHOCKING Experiment

Stanley Milgram said, "Life can only be understood backwards, but must be lived forwards." Milgram was a psychologist and professor at Yale best known for his experiments on obedience done in the 1960's. Besides the fact these experiments got him into a little hot water, their findings were profound and are still talked about to this day. He was trying to figure out why German soldiers sent millions of Jews to their deaths, all based on orders. His experiment was genius.

* Two People
* One teacher, one student
* If the student answers a question wrong, they get an electric shock

What the participant playing the teacher didn't know was that the student was one of the experimenters. At the beginning, the person playing the teacher would receive a minor electric shock so they could feel what would happen to the person playing the student when they answered incorrectly. They were asked to rate the strength of the electric shock. Most guessed really high, but the strength was only 45 volts.

As the experiment dragged on and the student answered the questions wrong on purpose, the voltage increased all the way to 450 volts. Surprisingly, even despite protests and begging to stop, the teacher participants continued to shock the student simply because a scientific authority figure commanded them to. When asked why they continued the shocks, most participants could not answer sufficiently.

They REALIZED that they were hurting and possibly even killing the other person (there were some points in the experiment where the student stopped responding to the questions and the shocks, yet the teacher kept increasing the voltage of the shocks when verbally commanded by the scientific authority figure) but did not ACT by stopping the experiment and walking out.

It's a part of our psyche we develop over time. It's called authority or power and it's completely imaginary. You can't see it, or measure it. All you know is when you're young; you listen to your parents. As you go through school you listen to your teachers or sit in detention. As you get older you listen to the boys in blue with guns and batons because they have the power now.

Every single subject had the power to use his or her own two feet and walk right out of the experiment, but the power of the man in the white coat overshadowed that. Once again, it's not logical, it's psychological and we need to figure out why.

Starting with WHY

Simon Sinek wrote a book called Start With Why (9), and in it explained that all people and businesses know WHAT they do, some of them may know HOW they do it, but very few of them know WHY. He developed a codex for this idea and calls it the golden circle.
Through this realization, Sinek is telling us that we need to communicate with each other from the inside out. No matter what you are trying to do in your life, people don't buy WHAT you do; they buy WHY you do it. The basis of any relationship is to attract people that believe what you

believe, not simply to attract people that like what you have, or what you can do for them.   This can be very difficult for us to do sometimes. Have you ever asked yourself why you chose the friends you have? Or why you stay away from or avoid other people?   It is all based on what biologists call fear conditioning.

Sinek explains this by saying that if you are looking at the brain from the top down, and slice it in half horizontally, the brain, and the way it operates fits perfectly into his golden circle.

There are 3 sections to the brain, and in order to understand this, I want you to think of it like a jelly-filled donut. The Neocortex is on the outside of the brain and corresponds with the "What" level of our actions. It represents the doughy part of the donut, makes us rationalize, analyze, and produces speech. The Limbic brain however, comprises of the middle two levels of the golden circle, and is like our jelly filling. Let's think about this for a second: the only reason you buy a jelly-filled donut is for the jelly. WHY? Because that's the good stuff! The limbic brain does all of the decision-making for us, regulates our behavior, and yet has no capacity to produce language.
Sinek says:

"When we communicate from the inside out we talk directly to the part of the brain that drives behavior. This is where our "gut" decision comes from. The part of the brain that controls decision-making doesn't control speech, and that's why something doesn't "feel" right."

What Sinek doesn't tell you is that deep inside that jelly donut is a little marble called the Amygdala. The amygdala is your panic button and it works very closely with your thalamus (also part of the limbic brain) to protect you from danger. The amygdala and thalamus are single neural link pathways, so they operate extremely fast. WHY do we need fast? For self-preservation! Imagine you just woke up and didn't even have your coffee yet. You put a pot on to brew and as you finish you look outside and see a nice fluffy Sunday morning newspaper sitting on the lawn. You walk outside rubbing your eyes half-awake, and as you bend down to grab the paper you see something curled up on the lawn out of the corner of your eye. This visual stimulus hits your thalamus, then shoots right to your amygdala. It's a snake says the amygdala! Jump back quick! But because you're in pajamas and slippers still you fumble around and fall backwards. As you are lying there, the information is finally passed onto the cortex and you see that the object your amygdala thought was a snake, was just a rolled-up garden hose.

This is the power these two structures have over our bodily control. They would much rather make you look foolish or clumsy, than be wrong and have you get bit and possibly die. And this is what happened to the people in Stanley Milgrim's experiment. The participants were paralyzed with fear by the illusion of power they thought the experiment controller had over them.

When asked, they could not explain WHY they kept going because the amygdala and the limbic system are not tied to speech, only fear/reaction. They knew pressing the button to shock the other person was wrong, but the fear of the imminent danger – the angry scientist – took precedence.

How many times do we get stuck in our lives feeling like we need to get out of a job, or out of a relationship, and yet we stay and don't know why? Fear of the unknown paralyzes us, even though our gut is telling us to run away as fast as possible. To combat this, we need to learn to trust our intuition more than the thinking mind. We need to realize this is happening for a reason. If you change and the outcome is better, great, but what if you make a change and the outcome gets worse? Those obstacles are there for you to learn and grow, but rather than face a new type of suffering, most of us will go back to suffering that's familiar.

To make change of this nature requires a large amount of reflection on our part. Asking yourself WHY you're doing what you are doing can open up some nasty doors to the human psyche. We may find out we have what some consider to be the wrong motives or values, but in some instances like the Wright brothers, we may also have the right values as well.

The Wright Values

In his TED Talk (9), Sinek gives a real-world example of what he means by starting with Why to have success in your life to get a true feeling of success or what we will learn is called Nishkama Karma. First he talks about Samuel Pierpont Langley, an American astronomer, physicist, and inventor who was given $50,000 to develop the airplane. He had a seat on the board at Harvard, worked at the Smithsonian institute, was a very well-connected man, and the New York Times followed him obsessively through this journey to accomplish flight. Everyone was rooting for this man.

On the other hand, you had the Wright brothers. They funded all of their experiments from the proceeds of their bike shop, they and their cohorts had no formal education, but what they did have was the BELIEF that flight would change the course of the world for the better and bridge the gaps between, time, distance and humanity.
Having a belief system explains to people WHY you are doing something, and when you talk to others about what you believe, you attract those that believe it! On December 17, 1903, the Wright brothers achieved manned flight and no one was there to report on it. Samuel Pierpont Langley had the wrong motivation from the get go, he simply wanted to be rich. Interestingly enough, he quit the day the Wright brothers took flight. Attracting people who believe what you believe compounds your time and energy through the Law of Diffusion of Innovation.

Innovation, It's What's For Dinner

The brain is designed to create, not to retain useless information that can be found by a simple Google search. Do you wonder why so few people access The Everspace? We have all heard of Newton's laws, most have heard of Murphy's Law, some have heard of Wolf's Law, yet I bet very few have ever heard of the Law of Diffusion of Innovation.

The law of diffusion of innovation goes something like this: there are a few of us that are lucky enough to use the brain to create something. Then, some people called the early adopters buy what you have created because they love to have everything first no matter what it is. Sinek says these are the people who will wait in line for 6 hours

just to get the new iPhone. Next come the early majority.
These people needed to get persuaded by a certain
number of early adopters to buy the product, and when
they do, the late majority and laggards follow suit after a
period of time.

Basically, what it comes down to is the first two groups
love having the newest things and the last three groups
just look for solutions and convenience. According to this
law, only 16% of people are willing to advance on blind
faith alone.

There is also something researchers call the Chasm. The
Chasm is between 15- 18% of the early adopters. Most
people or products make it to the 10% line and die out, but
when there's a push past the Chasm, major success is
guaranteed!

If you just talk about what you believe you will attract those
who believe it! Most innovators and early adopters are
comfortable making gut decisions while the rest of us are
not. They are driven by what they believe about the world,
Sinek says, and what you do, proves what you believe.
In my opinion, this Chasm can be linked to anything you
are thinking about doing in your life. On one side you
have complacency, then you have the Chasm, and on the
other side is greatness. Only about 10-15% of us get the
courage to make the leap. There's a great quote from
Meg Cabot that goes, "Courage is not the absence of fear
but rather the judgment that something is more important
than fear."

The problem is we are too complacent with our current
way of living to make that leap and live uncomfortably for a
while. For most of us, the grip of fear will only allow us to

look over the edge every once in a while, just to get a glimpse of what we COULD be doing. Some people want to dismiss the idea that everything happens for a reason and say we are not allowing ourselves to feel what we should feel in times of distress and are instead looking for false hope. I've done both; I've tried to accept and come to terms with the plight I have had in my life and it just does not provide the comfort searching for answers does, or connecting the dots like Mr. Jobs says.

Believing that everything happens for a reason gives us permission to not lead a perfect life. We're allowed to mess up because every mistake we make is another chance to learn. It's a life-school of which we are the student, the teacher, and the disciplinarian! I would rather dictate my own change in my life than sit around and wait for someone else to force me to do something I don't want to do.

To me, the closing of this lesson is bitter-sweet because I could use endless examples in my life and the lives of others that support connecting the dots in your past as to why you are where you are. Having said that, I'd like to leave you with this:

"The two most powerful warriors in life are patience and time." -Leo Tolstoy

Your Key to Accessing The Everspace: Faith VS. Trust

In order to access The Everspace we need gigantic amounts of faith. Faith showed me many times that I needed to have faith before I started to listen, so consider this a heads up.

Trust is not the same as faith. Once again, trust resides in the psyche; it's a thought form, while faith resides in the soul. Have you ever tried to explain why you have faith in something? It's impossible! That's because faith is a feeling! Connecting with this area of your soul daily is like saying, "Not my will be done Oh Lord, but thy will." You give up control and a lot of us have a huge problem with control.

When you trust someone and they break your trust, what happens? You get hurt, angry maybe, you stop talking to them for a while (or sometimes never again) and your relationship is never the same after that. You can't have a relationship with God or the Universe like that.
When I locked my heart and mind into faith, when I let go of thinking about how my life should be, my life unfolded magically right in front of me. I wake up every day free from concern knowing I'm being guided, instead of being paralyzed by fear of the next step.

Uncomfortability Challenge

Once a day feel extreme gratitude for someone you feel has wronged you. The best way to achieve this is to imagine they changed your life for the better, because in all likelihood, they probably did, but your negativity about the situation won't allow you to use their gift. Reflect on what happened and try to connect the dots like Steve Jobs says. The answer is there, look for it. Forgive them, and thank them. This can be silently, by e-mail, telephone, or if you're really up for an uncomfortable challenge, do it face to face!

Exercises

Think about an unusual, tragic, or surprising event. For each event, go through the questions below and write down all of your answers. This will help you better connect the dots and give you meaning to why these events had to happen in your life. We all play a part regardless of how much time we spend on the Earth.
1. Was there anything I learned that was useful from any of my life situations? About myself? About others? About other aspects of life?

2. Did I meet anyone as a result of good or bad situations either directly or indirectly that has played or will play a significant role in my life?

3. Did it lead to any beneficial changes in my life that would not have happened had I not experienced that life situation?

4. Did any situation in my life ultimately open any new doors, or provide any new opportunities?

References:

1. Covey, S. R. (1989). The seven habits of highly effective people: Restoring the character ethic. New York: Simon and Schuster.
2. Quinn, C. D. (Director). (2006). God Grew Tired of Us [Video file]. Retrieved from http://www.imdb.com/title/tt0301555/
3. McTaggart, L. (2008). The field: The quest for the secret force of the universe. New York: Harper.
4. Shadyac, T. (Director). (2010). I am [Video file]. Retrieved from http://www.iamthedoc.com/thefilm/
5. The Wachowski Brothers. (Director). (1999). The Matrix [Video file]. Retrieved from http://www.imdb.com/title/tt0133093/
6. Stanton, A. (Director), Stanton, A., Reardon, J., Burtt, B., Knight, E., & Garlin, J. (Writers), & Morris, J. (Producer). (n.d.). (2008). WALL-E [Video file].
7. Steve Jobs Stanford Speech
8. Coelho, P., Coelho, P., & Clarke, A. (1993). The alchemist. San Francisco: HarperSanFrancisco.
9. Simon Sinek Ted Talk - Start With Why

EverLesson 3: Live in the Now!

Day-

Noun: A period of twenty-four hours mostly misspent.

-Ambrose Bierce

The Fiction of Our Life

Even though it is lesson three, living in the Now is probably one of the greatest keys to accessing The Everspace because all life manifests in the present moment. For quite some time, my mind has been my worst enemy. My mind was a shit show. If things didn't go the way I wanted, if someone wasn't where they were supposed to be when they were supposed to be there, my imagination exploded and carried me over to a place that looked like Alice in Wonderland just met The Terminator. If I became agitated, the repetitive banter in my mind could last for weeks, even after amends to the situation were made. It just wouldn't stop. Accompanying this would be a nice pit in my stomach and a sharp burning in my solar plexus. I'd want to be somewhere else other than where I was. I'd want to just click my heels and disappear in a cloud of smoke. I had no idea how to make it stop and I started to hate myself for it.

If anyone was around me they were going to suffer too. My responses would be short, I wouldn't look them in the face, or if I was venting to someone, they felt the weight of what I was carrying. The emotions that I had trapped inside of me were building up into an H-Bomb and I swear when I went off there was going to be a blast radius of at least 50 miles.

Life does not exist outside of this current moment and that is where the fictional part comes in. The past, and the future are fantasylands, but our mind makes them out to be real. If there are two things I now know about these two fictional areas, it is this:

1. The past did not occur EXACTLY how you remember it.

2. The future is never as scary as your mind makes it out to be.

When it comes to the Now, I have two major teachers, Eckhart Tolle, and Ram Dass. If you're a spirit junkie like me, these guys need no introduction, as their expressions of the enlightenment they have received are profound to say the least. While they have published much information on the Now, we will focus on one key book by each and dissect their teachings to make this concept clearer and then I will expose my instruments for bringing me into the now. Nice guys always go last!

Depression Leads to Expression

Eckhart Tolle author of The Power of Now (1) had a magnificent awakening at the age of 29 when he was on the brink of a terrible depression. After this awakening, he quit studying for his doctorate and would sit for large amounts of time in parks, or on benches just observing the world move by. His family thought he had gone mad. Soon after he moved to the United States and started writing The Power of Now. Nearly broke and being without a publisher for his book, Tolle bought a lottery ticket and won $1000. That paid for his rent for the next month until a publisher picked up his book and the rest is history.

The Power of Now was published in 1999, and by August of 2000 was on the best sellers list. The unique aspect of the book is that he wrote it in question and answer format like a true teacher, rather than the book being like one big lecture. Even though it can get pretty dense at times, the message is clear as day.

80

Where is your attention focused for most of the day? As soon as you wake up, what is the first thought you have? Is it I'm hungry? I want coffee? My neck hurts? This meeting today is going to suck? Right from the get-go most of us are already missing the mark for the day. Our attention is dispersed, going into a thousand different directions. And then it gets worse.

Don't even try to check your e-mail, Facebook, or your bank statements because you will then get sucked into a totally different direction. Now it's "Why is this person emailing me again!?!?" I need to see what everyone else is doing because that is going to get me going. Ugh, my bank account is so depressing; if I just had more money everything would be ok.

At lunch you go further and further down the rabbit hole as you're scrolling through Instagram and you see a picture of your ex-boyfriend with some friends of his. Wait, does he have his arm around that skank? The emotions of him touching another girl just brought you to this one time 2 years ago when you thought he was cheating on you but it was just a misunderstanding, or was it. Now as you're sitting in this really important meeting that is all you can think about.

Tolle says we are like this because our "brains need content." If we don't fill it with what we want to think about, it is going to grab any memory, thought, emotion that it can coincide with the current moment and then use it to draw us elsewhere. This constant mental noise Tolle says, "comes in between you and your true self, you and all of your relationships, between you and nature, and

81

between you and God."

Think about it. How difficult is it to hear your friend talking to you at a concert? He or she can be standing right next to you and be screaming at the top of their voice and you'll still only catch 75% of what they're saying. This is what The Everspace has to compete with, except it will NOT raise its voice. It's your job to clear the space, quiet the mental noise, and hear its whispers. Once you do this the message becomes louder and louder and clearer and clearer until your mission or purpose in life unfolds like a map inside your head. You are now being guided; your brain is no longer the master, it is the servant, a medium between you and the Divine.

Are you really OK with being led to your purpose? Most people are not, Tolle says. We are raised in a society that says YOU get to choose. Let me assure you, there is no choice. If we could compile the names of everyone that wanted to be a professional athlete, but ended up selling insurance, or wanted to be an actor, but ended up waiting tables for a year then moving back home, or graduated with a psychology degree and then got a job in finance, there would be volumes and volumes to read.

Tolle says this is what happens when we live exclusively through memory and anticipation. "The past gives you identity and the future provides you with salvation." Do any of these examples sound like you?
- "I'd be so much better off if I never met such and such a person."
- "Once I get that promotion all of my money problems will go away."
- "My parents/teachers/coaches don't know what they are talking about and it irritates me."

- "People are so dumb, it's amazing."
- "People will respect me more when I get that Lexus."
Through most of what we call our "bad" experiences in life
we create what Tolle calls "pain bodies." Pain bodies are
essentially trapped life energy. For a moment we resisted
life and the message it was sending. All life is a
frequency, everything vibrates. As HeartMath proved, our
heart will actually pick up on this vibration first. If we react
negatively to this vibration it gets trapped, and now any
familiar event can trigger us into anxiety, or wanting
something else out of the current moment.
Michael Singer, author of The Untethered Soul: The
Journey Beyond Yourself (2) explains in beautiful detail
what is meant by that.

*"As you willfully struggle to keep these events from
passing through your consciousness, the energy first tries
to release by manifesting through the mind. This is why
the mind becomes so active. When the energy can't make
it through the mind because of conflicts with other
thoughts and mental concepts, it then tries to release
through the heart. In the yogic tradition, that unfinished
energy pattern is called a Samskara. This is a Sanskrit
word meaning "impression," and in the yogic teachings it is
considered to be one of the most important influences
affecting your life. A Samskara is a blockage, an
impression from the past. It's an unfinished energy
pattern that ends up running your life."*

Think about that for a moment. How many of us are afraid
to do something new, or even do something over again
because of a bad experience. Your redemption is sitting
right in front of you to experience something new and you
are paralyzed with fear, anxiety, anger, or sadness.
The bad news is this isn't even the bad news! If we don't

release these pain bodies or Samskara's, they will pile on top of each other. In common terms this is what we call emotional baggage. Singer says, "As a result, the protective energies have adapted toward defending the individual psychologically, rather than physiologically." When this occurs, we constantly live through fear bracing ourselves from moment to moment. Singer again, "When your heart is weak, it becomes susceptible to lower vibrations, and one of the lowest of all vibrations is fear. Fear is the cause of every problem. It's the root of all prejudices and the negative emotions of anger, jealousy, and possessiveness."

50 First Dates, One Huge Lesson

If you have never seen the movie 50 First Dates (3) I suggest you place it in your Netflix queue and pay careful attention. Drew Barrymore plays Lucy Whitmore and Adam Sandler plays Henry Roth. Henry is kind of like the player type, bouncing from one woman to the next until he meets Lucy and falls in love. The shocker comes when he meets Lucy for the second time and she has no recollection of who he is.

Confused, Henry asks around and finds out that she has short-term memory loss due to a car accident she suffered a few years back. Lucy can only remember something for 24 hours. Every time she goes to sleep, she wakes up not remembering what happened the day before. What, do you ask is the huge lesson? If you watch the movie, you will notice that every day Lucy wakes up she is incredibly happy. She has no ill will toward her family, or anyone she meets. She does not remember the accident; therefore she cannot play the role of the victim and continuously blame someone or something for her current state.

Only when she is made aware of the accident, and how much her father and brother do on a daily basis to ensure she doesn't find out does she become overwhelmed with grief. This got me thinking. Why can we not wake up like Lucy every day?

I'm not saying everyone should get a procedure to destroy their long-term memory, I'm saying why can we not wake up every day and be happy, even though we know people have wronged us? What if going to sleep was like clearing the trash on your computer. Every negative thought, every bit of spite you had for someone, your brain would find useless and just delete. This is what spiritual teachers do every day. It's called being centered.
Being centered doesn't mean I am expressionless or have no memory, it means I don't cling to them and cause them to define who I am and how I will react. Being centered is a promise to your heart and mind that I will treat every situation as new even if I believe I have lived it before and know how it's all going to play out.

The current moment is now. What am I doing right now? Suddenly our story becomes boring without the crap emotions, just as fictional books become boring without suspense. We keep turning the page because we NEED to KNOW what is going to happen.

Worrying about the future or regret for the past only arise if you kick yourself out of what you are doing now, and start creating the story of what you are going to do, or start re-reading the story of what was done in the past. Who wronged me before today? Which translates into, "who should I have anger for?" Who is going to wrong me in the future? Which translates into, "what enemies can I create?"

Answer this question: can you meet someone you already know without remembering their past or holding grudges about their past events? I bet for almost everyone reading this that seems like impossibility. Yet this is what we must do. I'm not saying to fall into another trap if someone is trying to manipulate you, you can remain open and loving and still tell someone no. I'm saying stop dwelling on it every second of the day because there are much more pleasant and productive things to think about.
Give up the stress of always fighting life, always complaining about this or that, or all the people who wronged you. Give up the cycling of the day's events before you try to fall asleep. Something happened in 1996 and that is why I can't be happy now. This person failed to do what they said they would and ruined my life, so I will dwell on it day after day to keep the pain going. Tolle says, "Life will give you whatever experience is most helpful for the evolution of your consciousness. How do you know this is the experience you need? Because this is the experience you are having at the moment."

Your personal history happened, no doubt about that. But the accumulation of these events is NOT who you are. They don't encapsulate you unless you personalize them. Forgiving someone does not mean you condone their actions; it means you are freeing yourself from being their emotional SLAVE.

Clock Time VS. Psychological Time

Clock time for the most part is simple. If my watch says 8 a.m., that means it's the same time as yesterday at this point, and it will be the same time tomorrow at this point and so on.

Psychological time on the other hand is a little bit tougher to grasp. Because we, as human beings, have the ability to think of the past and the future, our emotions will have the ability to control us, rather than us controlling our emotions. Here's Tolle on psychological time:

"How does this mind pattern operate in your life? Are you always trying to get somewhere other than where you are? Is most of your doing just a means to an end? Is fulfillment always just around the corner or confined to short-lived pleasures, such as sex, food, drink, drugs, or thrills and excitement? Are you always focused on becoming, achieving, and attaining, or alternatively chasing some new thrill or pleasure? Do you believe that if you acquire more things you will become more fulfilled, good enough, or psychologically complete? Are you waiting for a man or woman to give meaning to your life?"

He continues on and relates to how our emotions are controlled by psychological time:

"All negativity is caused by an accumulation of psychological time and denial of the present. Unease, anxiety, tension, stress, worry - all forms of fear - are caused by too much future, and not enough presence. Guilt, regret, resentment, grievances, sadness, bitterness, and all forms of non-forgiveness are caused by too much past, and not enough presence. The old patterns of

*thought, emotion, behavior, reaction, and desire are acted
out in endless repeat performances, a script in your mind
that gives you an identity of sorts but distorts or covers up
the reality of the Now. The mind then creates an
obsession with the future as an escape from the
unsatisfactory present."*

He said it perfectly, "A script in our mind." How many of
us have this script and when things don't go according to
the script we want to curl up and scream instead of
practicing flexible thinking. The point of this chapter is to
help you start living in the now. This present moment is all
we ever have, and sadness or anxiety can thrive only if we
allow it to by thinking about the past or the future and
judging it! That's right! So this brings us back to our first
two concepts. Is our perspective on the past and the
events that happened negative? If so we will be angry or
sad here in the present! That moment in time has come
and gone, yet by us reflecting negatively on it, and
refusing to find meaning, this moment can live within us as
if it is happening over and over every second of every day,
creating the deepest sadness, or the most profound anger.
We identify with these feelings and make them a part of
us, now they control us, instead of us controlling our
emotions.

Emotions like hate take control of our psyche and we stop
advancing in life. We shut people out. Opportunities fall
by the wayside. Even if someone tries to cheer us up, we
are more likely to bring him or her down because we make
what we feel so real, even though it no longer exists. Let
go of the past, and stop worrying about the future they are
both illusions. To do this we must cultivate the witness.

When the mind is the master, the ego gets cultivated to the max. The ego (which we will learn more of in lesson 5) is strictly concerned with the preservation of the self, which is mainly the physical body. This is the reason why so many of us fear death. Who are we without our body? Ask a bodybuilder and they would look at you confused. Who are we without our mind because surely that goes when we die? Ask any author and they would shudder at the thought of "losing" their mind.

The reality of it is we are neither. The body is the car, the brain is the engine.

But who's driving?

You are. The observer.

It took a long time to understand what Tolle and several other teachers meant by saying, "Be the observer," or "Cultivate the witness." As you become more present you realize you have the option of not having an opinion in any situation. You refuse to get aroused. You simply look on as if you are watching a play. When the actors get all riled up on stage, you don't butt in and yell, "Watch out Caesar! Brutus is going to kill you!" No, you simply remain quiet in your seat (Now I'm obviously not telling you to stand by and watch someone kill someone else, this is hypothetical mind banter I'm talking about).

The witness is one of neutrality. It knows nothing as Lao Tzu explain in the 37th line of the Tao Te Ching (4):

> *The Tao does nothing*
> *Yet leaves nothing undone.*

How simple of a concept, but yet it seems contradictory. How can something not do anything, but leave nothing undone? It's simple really. We need to stop forming opinions in our mind as to how life ought to go for us. Like I said before, we are raised in a society where we are told we have choice. Nature does not choose where trees are planted, which flowers bloom where, or how many fish are in the sea, yet all of these components find their way. A tree in Yosemite is not heard wishing it were growing in Brooklyn. Polar bears have no qualms living in the cold. They awaken every day and grow through their intuitive nature. Yet human beings awaken every day with a sense they have to DO something in order to prop up the universe and the illusion becomes it's not even you who is DOING the doing.

You don't have to save a couple's marriage. You don't have to help your friend battle out of depression. If the marriage is to be saved it will save itself. That will be the participant's path. If your friend is to break free from their depression, it will happen at the point in time when they are ready for that lesson. There's nothing we can do to expedite that. All we can do is be a glowing form of presence and observe.

Now again, this doesn't mean we are to sit at home and binge watch House of Cards (5). Cultivating the witness means developing love and empathy for others, but first and foremost developing an unwavering love for yourself. Someone can be upset and still be ok. You don't need to console them or bend to their every wish out of fear of upsetting them further. Nor should their attitude of anger, or hurt, or resentment influence your emotions and bring you down. This then breeds codependency.
We need to realize once again we have a "me" (your

90

brain), a "myself" (your body), and an "I" the infinite knowledge through which all life flows.

If you would like to learn more from Eckhart Tolle, you can go to:

https://www.eckharttolle.com

Or on twitter:
https://twitter.com/EckhartTolle

On Facebook:
http://www.facbook.com/Eckharttolle

On Instagram:
https://www.instagram.com/eckharttolle/

Ram Dass: A Stiff Back Leads to a Stiff Lesson

In the early 1960's Richard Alpert left his teaching position as a Psychology professor at Harvard University and decided to experiment with LSD. During his first experience, he saw a shadow of a person appear, and as he looked closer, he saw it was him as a Professor. As he focused on his own image, it then disappeared and he figured he was OK not being Richard the Professor anymore. The shadow then transformed into several other "self" images he knew to be him. Richard the pilot – gone, Richard the scuba diver – gone, Richard the lover – gone, but then as these images started to disappear, he happened to look down and saw that his legs were gone below the knee.

Alpert was OK with losing these images of himself, or who

he thought he was, but surely he couldn't lose his body, he NEEDED his body. Something interesting happened though as his body started to disappear. He was still aware, and this awareness knew, it really, really knew. This knowing created an irresistible urge in him to want to stay in that state ALL the time, but without LSD, this was impossible.

In the late 1960's Alpert found himself in India in search of this knowledge. He realized that turning this knowledge on superficially through drug use was not a means to an end. Coming down was depressing and he wanted to live in this state, not just visit it for short periods of time. One day through his travels, Alpert met a 23-year-old surfer from California named Bhagwan Dass. Even though he was so young, American, stood 6'7" tall and had long blond hair, Bhagwan was recognized as a "High" person in India. Alpert decided to follow this man in order to learn from him.   And learn he did.

Soon, Bhagwan Dass started to train him in a very interesting way and it started with his ability to live in the Now. Alpert would wake up after sleeping on the ground and complain about his hips or his back and Bhagwan would say, "Emotions are like waves, watch them disappear in the distance on the vast calm ocean." Then Alpert would try to tell him a story about a friend of his when he was at Harvard and Bhagwan would say, "Don't think about the past, just be here now." So Alpert would then ask him how long they were going to be on this trip and Bhagwan would say, "Don't worry about the future, just be here now." Alpert said that Bhagwan's presence just, "wiped out" his whole game. He was a great storyteller and was good at expressing emotions and so it became his nature to live everywhere besides the present moment. Because Bhagwan wasn't interested in all of the extraordinary dramas Alpert collected over his lifetime, his story started to disappear and a beautiful transformation occurred.

Be Here Now

The biography of Richard Alpert is beyond the scope of this book. There is however, one more piece to this puzzle. Once Alpert decided to stay in India and learn from his guru, he was appointed the name Ram Dass, which means "Servant of God." As Ram Dass continued to immerse himself into this spiritual world, he came back to the United States and started to talk and write about what he had discovered through his teachings and meditations. In 1971 he published his first book called Be Here Now (5).

The book was transformative to say the least and really made a statement in the realm of psychology, and spiritual expansion. Since then he developed the Love, Serve, Remember foundation, which has become a phenomenal resource for me. I highly suggest everyone reading this click through his site and read as many articles as you can. His podcast is an amazing series of talks that he gave when he got back from India all throughout the United States. Some of my favorite episodes are:

* The Thinking Mind
* More Profound Than Miracles
* Edge of the Mystery
* Dharmic Fire
* Smorgasborg
* Veil of Tears

93

* Trust, Contentment, and the Guru
* Separation, Lust, and Kali

And there are many, many more. The challenge of living in the present moment Ram Dass says, or what most people call the "Now" is dealing with the power the thinking mind has over us.

The first step is realization or awareness, and then it is bridging the gap between realization and application. For years I knew the best way to be happy was to simply be present, but my thinking mind simply wouldn't have it. The funny part about it was I read so many books by so many other authors, and it was really only the title of Be Here Now that I had to read.

I feel the cleverest solutions to problems are always the simplest as well and for me to break the cycle it was as easy as reminding myself every time I started to complain or having negative self-talk to "BE HERE NOW" just as Bhagwan Dass kept suggesting.

Decondition the Mind, Air Condition the Spirit

What does deconditioning the mind mean? Quite plainly, it means to erase all of the habitual no's and habitual yes's that occur in our day-to-day life. Once again, we do this by treating every event in our life as if we are experiencing it for the first time. Does this mean we touch a glowing orange stove to see if it is hot? NO! Commonsense here, people. What it means is we keep our HEART open to others at all times. Closing yourself off to others does not allow for the natural flow of life and distracts our attention from what is happening right NOW.

For this section, we are going to use relationships as an example of living in the now. During one of his teachings, Ram Dass was talking about his guru teaching everyone about keeping your heart open at all times, even to hurt and suffering which, for most of us is extremely hard to do. The way to enlightenment is to love everyone, and everything, to see the world as being divinely orchestrated and perfect, even during tragic events or what we would perceive to be negative occurrences. One day Dass' guru caught a student stealing butter from the home they were all living in, and he was selling it to make a profit. The guru became extremely irate and yelled at the student to leave and never come back. Ram Dass questioned his guru, stating, "I thought you are supposed to keep your heart open to everyone?" The guru responded, "You can throw someone out of your life, just never throw them out of your heart."

I thought this was a very profound point because for most people, you're either in, or you're out. How difficult is it to still have love for someone who has wronged you? How challenging is it not to respond to hurt with hate? To suffering with disgust? To pain with wanting to show that person how much pain they caused you?
By responding in this way, we block our ability to GROW spiritually and become a better person. Ram Dass is a huge believer in reincarnation and believes these hardships are a result of Karma, and a way to release what is clinging to our spirit. If you have a problem with trust, you'll always be paranoid. If you have a problem with jealousy, you'll constantly have things taken from you until you give it up.

Avoiding these situations prevents the opportunity for us to practice deconditioning our mind to programmed responses, and believe me; this takes A LOT of practice. There are a few considerations that we can look at that can break the conditioning of how we would normally react in certain situations in our relationships that may prevent us from living in the now. First is loving someone with all of your heart, truly loving them, but performing an action that hurts them FOR their own good.

Remember, things don't happen TO us, they happen FOR us. An example in my own life is my decision to divorce my wife. She left me and could not decide whether she wanted to be married, or get divorced. After 10 roller-coaster months, our relationship was becoming seriously toxic. I kept looking at old pictures, thinking about how happy I was, and would daydream about how scared I would be in a future without her. I was living everywhere except where I needed to be, which was here and now! Even though I still loved her, and as much as I wanted things to work out, I asked for the divorce in order to break this vicious cycle so we could BOTH start to or continue to grow again. Life is not meant to be lived at a standstill; if you are not growing, you are moving backwards. This leads me into learning how to love with conditions.
We are CONDITIONED by society that we should love our significant others unconditionally. Well, I'm saying you should never love someone unconditionally. Ram Dass said we were born from unconditional love, we are here to experience the conditions of it!

I am the only one I am aware of that will actually admit to people that I have conditions for love, and the reason I have these conditions is because I respect myself, and love myself. The statement, "I'm happy if you're happy" breeds codependency and is a recipe for disaster. By denying your feelings, you're missing your appointment for life, for honesty, to be real and raw with someone you respect, and believe me, someone will explode. You are, in a sense, putting that emotion on the back burner and waiting to deal with it at a later date. Have you ever gotten into an argument with your significant other, and then 10 minutes into the argument you realized you have argued about everything that's wrong in your relationship besides the initial point that was brought up? After, you left confused and uncertain about what even happened? You were both living somewhere else.

You should not suffer to see someone else happy, that is a one-way street. If a decision someone made, or an action someone took was against you, and you don't agree with it, you must let it be known because you are setting yourself up to be a doormat. This is called a love trap. People who love each other still hurt each other but it is done on accident. If someone who says they love you is hurting you in a vindictive way, then that IS NOT LOVE! To know The Everspace requires great amounts of internal strength to perform the tasks you will be given. Can you look at someone with all the love in your heart and tell him or her the answer is NO? I'm serious. Can you look at someone and have no ulterior motive other than "no means no, and I still love you."

So many of us are people-pleasers. We lie to ourselves to preserve the peace we are experiencing now, but will eventually explode with irritation later on. We are conditioned to feel an answer of no is a reduction to our being. When we continually say yes to others when we mean no, the only person we are reducing is ourselves. Our values no longer hold weight and we become a pushover.

Relationships are challenging and require a ton of work on both sides for them to succeed, I understand that. Extreme presence is what gets us through the challenging parts and helps us enjoy the good times that much more. In Tim Ferriss' book The Four-Hour Work Week (6) he suggests doing a two-day experiment where every response you have is no. Break the conditioning of being a people-pleaser, and break the cycle of people using you. You don't have to make up elaborate lies when saying no, just ask people to respect your position and move on. Living in the now means learning how to deal with our emotions. Once our memory ties an event to an emotion, it's got us and can consume our every breath. I've been there, and I'm sure you have too. Ram Dass tells us that in order to stay present, treat emotions like insects flowing down a river.

Imagine you are standing on the bank of a river. As you see an insect pass you notice it, but you do not think about it much longer after it passes. You certainly don't think about it the next day. When we latch on to our emotions, more importantly when we IDENTIFY with them, we are no longer living in the current moment, we are caught up in wanting a better past or hoping for a better future and those are predicaments the mind has no tools to create anything positive with.

Your Key to Accessing The Everspace:

Mastering the Art of Consciousness: Attention, Presence, and Surrender

Mastering the art of being conscious does not mean you have to move to Tibet and convert yourself into a Zen master. There are three principles we need to master and realize which situation calls for which tool.

Attention is easy. You've heard your mom or teacher yell at you to pay attention and what do you do? You stiffen up and listen to the rest of what they are saying. As soon as they are done, you go back to goofing off. Here's another example. Say you're at Grandma's house and you just finished dinner. As you're helping her do the dishes afterwards she starts telling you about her knitting club that she just joined. You're paying attention, you're listening, but it's not like you have to stop washing dishes, turn toward your grandmother and focus on what she is saying in order to be respectful or respond. Your mind can handle the job just fine. Which brings me to our next principle, presence.

Presence goes a little deeper than attention. Let's pretend your parents, or significant other want to talk to you about something that is troubling them deeply. That is not a time to be on your phone, playing video games or reading a magazine.

This is a situation that in order for the accusing party to walk away with a sense of accomplishment requires the use of both your heart and your mind. Turn the phone off, pause the game, or put the magazine down. Focus on what they are saying and rather than defending yourself, learn to take their concerns and use it to self-reflect before bed, or during a meditation.

Keeping your heart and your mind open can help to reduce any negative emotions that might arise out of the conversation. Successful people know that they are never as bad as people make them out to be, but also do not believe that they are some sort of demigod when praised.

Presence brings strength to any situation, no matter how difficult to grasp or swallow, and will prevent you from shutting down, or escalating the conversation into anger. There's a sentence I use to snap me back into presence. Sometimes I might be walking, or reading, or sitting and my mind will drift to something that happened 6 months or even a year ago. As that grabs my attention, I say in my head, "Dude where are you right now?" I know it sounds silly, but it really does the trick for me and had enhanced my ability to stay present, even in my downtime.
Surrender is one of the most difficult tasks to master and is something I still work with this day. If attention is using your mind, and presence is using you heart AND mind, then surrender is using your heart, your mind, and your soul to focus on the outcome of any moment life throws at you.

Remember, you always have the option of no opinion in any situation in life. Society conditions us though to label things as either bad or good. I was flying out to Johannesburg from Atlanta International Airport, and while waiting at my gate noticed a woman at the desk. She was sobbing and pleading and looking around at everyone with streams of tears running down her face. Her flight had been cancelled due to Hurricane Matthew coming through. Now I didn't know her situation, or what her life had been like, but the wanting and desire of that woman to get on a plane and head toward a natural disaster was to me downright silly. This was far beyond the reach of anyone at Delta. I understand emotion and all that but this woman was digging herself deeper and deeper into a victimized state by the minute while her presence of mind could have been directed elsewhere. In a case like this we need to surrender to what is. We need to completely accept what is and not let our emotions be affected by not getting what we want.

To learn the capacity to surrender there's a mantra I use every morning to prepare myself for the chaos of what every day may bring.

"You must accept everything that happens in your life today as if you have chosen it yourself."

If you want to enter The Everspace, I urge you to make this part of your practice.

Uncomfortability Challenge:

Scientists have shown that when we engage with social media or our cell phones, a hormone in our body called dopamine is released (7). Sex, alcohol, tobacco, drugs, and gambling all release dopamine; it is our reward hormone so to say.

With all of the apps, email notifications, and text messages our brain is on a constant dopamine high all day long. This amount of overstimulation creates addiction. Eating out with a spouse used to be a very intimate event in the 1950's. You may run into someone you know, but it was highly unlikely. Now you can go to dinner with 500 contacts in your pocket and 37,000 followers on 5 different social platforms. Everyone has something to say, and you must keep up with it all for "fear of missing out (FOMO)." Your partner now has to compete with the thoughts of close to 38,000 other people. Every buzz, bing, or tone creates more and more anxiety as they fear losing your attention to a little black box.

101

Being unfriended, blocked or banned on some of these platforms can cause extreme devastation to our self-confidence and self-worth. A friend of mine broke up with his girlfriend but remained friends and followed her on Facebook. As he saw her living her life and starting to date again, anger, sadness, and confusion began consuming his life. He tried unfriending her but just couldn't pull the trigger no matter how much courage he tried to develop.

What did he do?

He combatted one dopamine trigger with another. My friend ended up getting really drunk one night by himself and then finally cut the cord and blocked her. He told me it was like breaking up with her all over again. The problem this generation is facing is that in times of emotional distress or need, they are turning to a device rather than a person to find answers.

My uncomfortable challenge to you is four-fold and I urge you do this one in steps.

1. Disable all notifications on your phone for all of your social media platforms.
2. Delete the Facebook, and Twitter app from your phone. You may leave Instagram since it is a mobile-only platform; just make sure to keep the notifications turned off. You won't die if you can post to Facebook via desktop only. Trust me, your ancestors did it back in 2001.
3. Unsubscribe from e-mails that are cluttering your inbox or that are trying to sell you something. A bonus would be to clean your inbox of old messages up until one week ago. File important e-mails in folders.
4. Delete pictures of old relationships and unfriend

toxic/negative people. This is where many of you may draw the line. But how am I going to remember?!?! Or what if I see him or her in real life. I've had people drop me in real life because I unfriended them on social media and let me tell you, my life IMPROVED. Sometimes the hand we hold that holds us down is our own.

Exercises
Write down a goal along with three ways you can achieve it every day, week, month and year.

Goal:

Daily way to achieve:

Weekly way to achieve:

Monthly way to achieve:

Year-end goal to achieve:

If you are unhappy right now with a current life situation, write down what is keeping this feeling alive. Then write down the purpose for keeping this feeling alive. If there is no purpose, let it go and start living in the now.

Write down what you are resisting in your life. For example, you don't want to do homework, you hate cleaning your room or helping your little brother with chores. Look at the situations you wrote down and practice flexible thinking in the NOW by finding ways to better cope with these situations when they do arise.

Example: I hate taking out the garbage.

Flexible thinking solution #1: I will put my iPod on and play my favorite song at the time while I take out the trash.

Solution #2: I will make the bags as heavy as possible and turn it into a mini training routine, trying to beat my time every day I do it.

References:
1. Tolle, Eckhart. The Power of Now: A Guide to Spiritual Enlightenment. Novato, CA: New World Library, 1999. Print.
2. Singer, Michael A. The Untethered Soul: The Journey beyond Yourself. Oakland, CA: New Harbinger Publications, 2007. Print.
3. 50 First Dates. Dir. Peter Segal. By George Wing. Perf. Adam Sandler, Drew Barrymore, Rob Schneider. N.p., n.d. Web. 2004.
4. Tzu, Lao. Tao Te Ching. Milano: Mondadori, 2001. Print.
5. Dass, Ram. Be Here Now. San Cristobal, NM: Lama Foundation, 1971. Print.
6. Ferriss, Timothy. The 4-hour Work Week: Escape 9-5, Live Anywhere, and Join the New Rich. Chatham: Vermilion, 2011. Print.
7. @ama_marketing. "Social Media Triggers a Dopamine High." Social Media Triggers a Dopamine High. N.p., n.d. Web. 08 Nov. 2016

EverLesson 4.
Nishkama Karma

"No man is crushed by misfortune, unless he is first deceived by prosperity."

-Lucius Annaeus Seneca

Frejus, France

Don't DO Good, BE Good

The laws of Karma are inescapable to those who believe in it. Karma in a literal sense is every action we perform as human beings. Walking, talking, praying, breathing, thinking, everything physical or mental is considered Karma and each action leaves a mark on us.
Dharma is another law that is inescapable to those that believe in it. There is no single word that defines Dharma and there are many different meanings given to it depending on which Indian religion you follow. For argument's sake, when we use the word Dharma, we will be talking about the "right way of living." In a metaphysical sense, Karma is the action, and Dharma is the path. In a physical sense, Karma is the body, and Dharma could be considered the mind.

This is a common practice in Eastern Philosophy, but creates much conflict when we try to adapt it to Westernized living. In America we are taught from a very young age that when you do something, you "deserve" something in return. One of the issues that are arising now that thankfully I did not have to deal with in my generation is the issuing of participation trophies. When I was growing up, places first through third got a trophy, and any team after that got bupkis.

By issuing these participation trophies we teach our young that no matter what you do in life, you are going to get something back in return. An easy term we can think about to help make the connection is entitlement. Lost becomes the idea of working in a soup kitchen, or doing

108

community service. Lost becomes the idea of stories like the Good Samaritan. Lost becomes the idea of even helping a friend move.

When I was running a CrossFit gym I took an online business course about selling memberships and was introduced to the acronym WIIFM. The instructor asked if we knew what that meant and I was dumbfounded. I thought it was an Instagram hashtag. He then went on to explain it means "What's In It For Me." I was shocked. He told us that in order to generate more sales we need to explain why exercise is beneficial to a potential member. To my mental constructs this was incredible. Explain why exercise is beneficial? I thought it was obvious.
There's no denying that this is the world we now live in. Some want to say it's failed parenting and I could see that. I've been to many lacrosse, baseball, and football practices where I watch 30-something-year-old parents sitting on their cell phones while their kids play their hearts out. My parents were always at my practices, hell, my Father even coached my team for a couple years, but I digress.

While most of what we just talked about has no bearing on this lesson, what it does do is set the stage for one of the utopian ideas I spoke about in my introduction, and that is the idea of Nishkama Karma, or more commonly called Karma Yoga. To first introduce this concept, we will use a story.

There was a holy man who used to practice meditation sitting on the bank of a river. One day he saw a scorpion being carried away by the current of the river. Out of compassion he grabbed hold of it and released it on the ground. As soon as he touched the scorpion it stung his

hand, causing him terrible pain.
After a while the scorpion fell back into the water and was again about to be carried away by the current. Again, the monk rescued it and was stung by the ungrateful creature. A third time the scorpion fell into the river, and seeing its pitiable condition, the compassionate monk started to rescue it.

At that moment, a bystander said to the monk: "Sir, I have been watching you. I saw how that scorpion stung you several times. Still you are trying to save its life?"
The monk replied: "The nature of a scorpion is to sting, and the nature of a holy person is to do good to others, so I am following my nature. It is true the scorpion stung me, but that does not mean I must be cruel."
Saying so, the monk picked up the scorpion once more and carried it to a distant place so that it could not again fall in the water (1).

I know what you're thinking. That guy is soooooooo dumb right! I mean who in their right mind would continue to pick up a scorpion after it kept stinging him. After all it is just a scorpion, he should have just let it float on down the river and die. But that's not the point if you are a believer of Nishkama Karma, which is the fourth lesson we need to adhere to in order to be welcomed into The Everspace.

The Swami Says

Swami Vivekananda was an Indian Hindu Monk who lived in the late 1800's and was the chief disciple of the 19th century saint Ramakrishna. Vivekananda is credited with introducing Hinduism and yoga to the western world. Many of his talks were transcribed and turned into books that still get sold to this day.

In his book, Karma Yoga: The Yoga of Action (2), he lays out a road map (Dharma) for what one would consider their life's work and it is a complete 180-degree shift from what we are taught in school growing up in the West. Many people want to discount that knowledge by saying it just isn't relative in today's economy but I tend to disagree. People in his day lived a much quieter lifestyle than we do today without cell phones, cars, and alarms and could "hear" the message of intuition much clearer. He goes on to describe Karma's many key aspects on the nature of our soul.

In chapter 1 - Karma in its Effect on Character, he states that as human beings evolve we start to realize it is knowledge we are after, not happiness. He contends that all knowledge comes from the inside, but is stimulated by the outside. That the external world in which we live day to day gives us subtle suggestions to remember what we already know. We are not learning per se, but discovering our truth as we get older and experience more and more. In Karma Yoga, all work is simply there to bring out the power of the mind to wake up the soul. Enlightenment is not knowledge we are obtaining, it is knowledge we are remembering and that is why it can also be called "Awakening."

The moral principle of Karma Yoga states that we "have the right to any type of work we want, but we do not have the right to the fruits there of." To Western society this is an absurd way of thinking. If I work hard I better get paid for it and somebody better damn well notice the amazing job I did. If not, what did I do it for? I see it often in our youth who need constant reinforcement of the great job they had done. I hear stories of kids misbehaving in school and parents then reprimanding the teacher for reprimanding their perfect child. If I got in trouble in school, I got in trouble at home as well. It was just that simple.

If I had to develop a Karmic law for The Everspace it would be this, "The Everspace does not care how you do what it is asking you, and it even does not care if you complete the task, it will simply move the idea on to someone else." If the Divine asks you to not have expectations from your work, how can it have expectations of its work?

Rather than the 10 commandments, there are only two laws those who believe in Karma must abide by.

1. Every unselfish action is good
2. Every selfish action is bad.

If you're performing a task for a reward or praise, then ultimately that is a selfish action. We all need to make money in order to live, that is not what he is talking about here. You can go to your day job and ask for a raise if you feel like you are underpaid. The tasks being referred to are the mental constructs we create as to how we feel the world should work. Vivekananda says,
"In the first place, a man who can work for 5 days, or even for 5 minutes, without any selfish motive whatever, without thinking of future, of heaven, of punishment, or anything of the kind, has in him the capacity to become a powerful moral giant. It is hard to do it, but in the heart of hearts we know its value and the good it brings. It is the greatest manifestation of power – this tremendous restraint; self-restraint is a manifestation of greater power than all

outgoing action."

That's pretty terrifying stuff. This totally erases the theories on intention and the basic notions of Karma where I feel if I do good, or if I help this person, that the good deed will bring fortune to me in the future. Did you ever hear of someone loaning somebody a thousand dollars and then that person never pays them back? The person who lent the money then says, "That's ok, I know it will come back to me." This seemingly selfless act – the act of forgiving a loan of your hard-earned money – is still considered selfish if you believe the Universe will look kindly upon you when you next need it most. To Karma Yoga standards you are still wrong.

What do we do then? We give it up. We detach from the benefit any work, or help we do on our behalf for another being or the rest of humanity. Even believing that you are the doer of the work that is being done is bondage and therefore not Karma yoga. We are all mediums through which the divine acts we are not the creators.

We can see this depicted well in the movie The Man Who Knew Infinity (3). It is the story about a young Indian man named Ramanujan who from a simple math text was able to extrapolate theories that upset many mathematicians because there was simply no proof to his conclusions. Ramanujan knew that what he was writing down was true and wanted to get his work published feverishly so he would send out letters to Colleges in hopes that someone would see his genius and bring him over to publish his work. A man by the name of G. H. Hardy who was a Professor at the Trinity College in Cambridge soon realized his genius and brought Ramanujan over to further his computations. However, the College's Professors

113

denounced every new theory that Ramanujan came up with and one day demanded to know where he was getting them. His answer? God. This created further problems because now to the Professors Ramanujan looked like a trickster, and Mr. Hardy looked like the tricked.

Eventually, as Ramanujan's theorems prove to be correct, Hardy elects him for a fellowship. He is unsuccessful the first time, but succeeds remarkably the second. During his discourse on why Ramanujan should be accepted, the writers do something interesting. Hardy is shown throughout the entire film as being an atheist, and even comments at the end that "the only romantic relationship he ever knew was with Ramanujan." In his speech to the Fellowship council, Hardy's notions of God and the divine soften for a bit when he defends Ramanujan's claims that he gets his theories from God. Hardy says,

"He told me that an equation for him had no meaning unless it expressed a thought of God.
Well, despite everything in my being set to the contrary, perhaps he is right. For is this not exactly our justification for pure mathematics?
We are merely explorers of infinity in the pursuit of absolute perfection. We do not invent
these formulae, they already exist and lie in wait for only the very brightest of minds, like Ramanujan, ever to divine and prove. So, in the end, I have been forced to consider, who are we to question Ramanujan, let alone God?"

This illustrates Vivekananda's points very well. All knowledge is contained in the infinite. Our minds are the mediums through which we remember this knowledge. Ultimately, when we put the knowledge into practice, we must not "Think" we are the ones doing the work.

By understanding the tenets of Karma Yoga, we have now laid the groundwork for how this great, infinite knowledge works. It is not driven by reward; it is driven by BELIEF. All you have to do is believe in The Everspace and you are granted access. The problem is two-fold though. You either don't know about this space because you have not been taught very well, or you have this hunch, this little pecking in your mind, your heart or your soul, giving you all of these ideas, but you dismiss them as pure rubbish. How many times has a thought popped in your head but then you think, "Naw, I could never do that." This is because The Everspace does not discriminate! This is what was meant when Jesus said, "We are all equal in the eyes of God."

If knowledge is simply accumulated through experience, then how do you explain people like Ramanujan? Or Mozart? Or Picasso? Or Blaise Pascal? We've already heard the story about Ramanujan, but did you know that Mozart wrote his first symphony at age 8? That Picasso was thinking about painting before he could even speak? Or that Pascal was studying geometry in the 1600's against his father's will at the age of 12? When his father found out he was shocked that his son had recomposed the theories of Euclid and thus began taking him to weekly meetings with elite mathematicians in Paris. To slam-dunk my point, have you ever heard of Pascal's Wager? It's a philosophical bet created by Mr. Pascal, which states that believing in God costs you nothing if you are wrong, but everything if you are right. And that's my guarantee to you, believing in The Everspace will cost you nothing if I am wrong. There's no membership fee (besides the price of this book) or sacrifices associated with joining this elite group of creatives. If I'm wrong you can still keep your job at Microsoft, Chevron, or Abercrombie and Fitch, but if I'm right, and you do everything I say in this book, you'll be living your true purpose here on Earth, and you will become happier than you have ever imagined.

Real Life Models of Nishkama Karma

Before we get into some extraordinary stories of these models, there's some sciencey stuff we need to discuss first. I love science. Being a Strength and Conditioning coach for 18 years, I considered myself to be an experimenter of the human body. Like I said in my introduction, in my early 20's I became agnostic. I was doing all of this research on the body and figured that science had everything figured out. So why believe in God? There's nothing mystical going on here, it's just cells and chemical reactions. That all changed when I read McTaggart's book, The Field. That book bridged the gap between science and God for me. It showed that what science is studying is God. Just like G. H. Hardy said in his defense of Ramanujan, they are all pursuing the infinite. What is infinite? God is infinite. All mathematicians are looking for this one equation that is absolute and explains everything in numbers; scientists are doing experiments to explain everything in words. In my opinion they need to choose their words a little more carefully.

Neurosciency Stuff

Your brain is the medium through which The Everspace helps you manifest its ideas. To understand how this occurs, we first need a short crash course on how the brain perceives the external world.

There are two hemispheres we need to be concerned with, the right and the left. The right hemisphere is connected to the left eye, and concerned with creativity, and the left hemisphere is connected to the right eye and concerned with language. You can see this in the picture below.

Right Brain Functions	Left Brain Functions
Art Awareness	Analytic Thought
Creativity	Logic
Imagination	Language
Intuition	Reasoning
Insight	Writing
Music Awareness	Numbers
Left-Hand Control	Right-Hand Control

Right in-between both parts of the brain are a dense series of nerve fibers called the corpus callosum that allows both sides to communicate. In medicine, there are certain cases where all other modalities fail in mental illness and doctors actually go in and cut the corpus callosum in order for the patients to stop having seizures and the like. These people actually live a pretty normal life, but when you now retest their cognitive abilities with the hemispheres severed (split brain) you start to learn a lot more about how the brain works as a whole.

David McRaney wrote a book titled You Are Not So Smart: Why You Have Too Many Friends on Facebook, Why Your Memory Is Mostly Fiction, and 46 Other Ways You're Deluding Yourself (4). In it he talks about how split-brain patients have been studied since the 1950's and the researchers have come up with interesting results. If you look at the picture of the brain again, you'll see the left brain controls language, but the right brain controls creativity. So if you have an idea for a new product, how does this come out in split-brain individuals? Very weirdly, as we will find out.

Psychologist Michael Gazzaniga at The University of California at Santa Monica was one of the first to study the limitations of these split-brain individuals. In one experiment, subjects looked at a cross in the middle of a computer screen and then the word "truck" was flashed on the left side of the screen only. Now the right side of the brain should have picked that up and communicated to the left side of the brain to tell the vocal cords to say truck, but when asked, the split-brain subjects couldn't say anything. They didn't know. What is even more amazing is when these subjects were given a pencil and were asked to draw what they had seen with their left hand, they easily doodled a truck. If you look at the diagram of the brain again, you will see that the right-side brain controls the left hand.

Now let's take a step back. Swami Vivekananda talked about Karma Yoga and the outside being a stimulus for what our mind needs to remember. This is how we learn. Your brain is doing this all-day long. Both sides are talking to each other; the new experiences are stored away, and the repetitive ones like turning a key are already ingrained so they are discarded. But what about if we want to create something like a painting, or build a tree house, or write a song? There's one key factor that scientists just discovered.

The Magic of Bob Dylan

In May of 1965, Bob Dylan was on tour and it was not going very well for him. The fans were raving about his songs, the venues were packed, and the news people and cameramen were constantly in his face asking him how he came up with such amazing songs. What isn't going well you ask? It was at that point where Dylan was considering quitting the music business.

Dylan was burned out from touring so much and playing songs that he just didn't like. He was sick of the questions about where he got the ideas for his songs, or what his great message was because he just didn't know. He wrote and made music because that's all he knew how to do and he was sick of all the attention. In his book, Chronicles: Volume One (5) he says,
"People think that fame and riches turn into power, that it brings glory and honor and happiness. Maybe it does, but sometimes it doesn't. I found myself stuck in Woodstock, vulnerable and with a family to protect. If you looked in the press, though, you saw me being portrayed as anything but that. It was surprising how thick the smoke had become."

His amazing talent was being ruined by fame, but as we know, Bob Dylan would persevere.

In an article written by Jonah Leher entitled: The Neuroscience of Bob Dylan's genius (6) we pick up where Michael Gazzaniga left off with a man named Mark Beeman, a young scientist at the National Institute of Health in the early 1990's. Beeman was studying people

119

who specifically had damage to the right side of their brain. These patients would come in and they would talk about how their doctor said how lucky they were because the right side of the brain is barely used and it's not responsible for language and so on. Besides those statements, Beeman still saw that these people had some pretty serious cognitive problems. Some of these people couldn't understand jokes, or sarcasm or metaphors, and others had a really hard time looking at a map or deciphering a painting.

Being intrigued with this, Beeman set up a study. He theorized that the right side of the brain, which is the creative side, would take over after the left side of the brain (analytical side) ran out of options. For instance, saying something like, "Give a baby a hammer and the whole world becomes a nail" to people who do not have right brain damage does not mean that the world literally turns into a nail. The left side picks up the language and the right side makes sense of this till you realize it is just a figure of speech. This doesn't happen for people with right-brain damage, and it seems metaphors are the hardest thing for them to pick up. What Beeman was starting to realize is that the right side of the brain helps us to build a subtle connection to unrelated things when a blatant answer is not staring us in the face.

The icing on the cake then was a talk Beeman was listening to in 1993 by a psychologist named Jonathan Schooler. Schooler had given subjects a problem. There is a heavy steel pyramid sitting upside down on a $100 bill. How do you remove the bill without moving the pyramid? He then hooked the subjects up to a funky set of goggles that allowed them to flash a word in one eye at a time. When they flashed the hint on how to solve the problem in the right eye (concerned with language) the subject wouldn't pick it up, but when they flashed the hint into the left eye (creating subtle connections) the answer came to them in an AH HA! sort of way (The answer is to burn the $100 bill). This is how our brain generates an insight.

Beeman now had better direction, but he needed to devise an experiment which sometimes provided insights to solve it and sometimes didn't. The puzzles he and partner John Kounios created were word plays. They would give the subjects three words like age, mile, and sand and ask them to figure out what single word would make them compound (In this case you would use Stone: Stone Age, Milestone, Sandstone). The subjects had 15 seconds to solve the puzzle, and if they did, they were to answer it the answer arrived by and insight or if they had to analyze it first.

Beeman and Kounios soon found what they were looking for. They realized that while it seemed like the insight answer came out of nowhere, the left hemisphere was actually paving the way for the right hemisphere to do its job. Within a few seconds the left side got tired and the subjects became frustrated before passing the task on to the right side. What's interesting is the frustration is an essential part of the creative process. How many times do you hear a story about someone being on the brink of quitting and then BAM the idea they were searching for popped into their brain like a magic lightning bolt? The frustration tells the right brain it better get to work to find alternatives for the answer we are seeking.

About 30 milliseconds before the insight arrives, Beeman and Kounios could measure a sudden burst of gamma wave rhythm coming from the anterior superior temporal gyrus (aSTG), a small fold of tissue, located on the surface of the right hemisphere just above the ear. This is named the "neural correlate of insight" and is where scientists believe our insight comes from.

You're going to remember that I said a little bit ago I would like to see science choose their words more carefully. As you can see, the word "from" is in bold in the previous paragraph; I would like to change that word to through. We need to start to look at the brain as a medium like I discussed before. It is a passageway to the infinite knowledge that the Universe is trying to share with us. We all have this ability. The insights depend on what niche we are in, what our passion is, or where our talents lie. For Bob Dylan, it was music.

Reading Chronicles: Volume One, you get a sense that Dylan was made up of two parts. He was one part Everspace, and one part Karma Yogic. He is found saying, "I really was never any more than what I was – a folk musician who gazed into the gray mist with tear-blinded eyes and made up songs that floated in a luminous haze." To me, it seemed like the man just wanted to make music and have those songs be what they are. He didn't want credit for how good they were, and he didn't want to explain them or where they came from because he didn't know.
In relation to The Everspace, Dylan, who rarely granted interviews spoke to Ed Bradley of 60 Minutes in 2004 and admitted that it wasn't him writing the songs (7). In the interview, Dylan recites the opening lyrics of "It's Alright, Ma" which go:

"Darkness at the break of noon

Shadows even the silver spoon
The handmade blade, the child's balloon
Eclipses both the sun and moon
To understand you know too soon
There is no sense in trying."

He then goes on to say that his early songs were almost magically written and he has no idea about how he came up with the lyrics. Mr. Dylan was tapping into The Everspace, because those songs needed to be written and this magic used him as a medium to bring it to the world.

To me, it seems as though Dylan wasn't aware of his powers. Once again, in his book he is found talking about how most singers tended to put the focus on them, and he wanted to put the focus on the songs. To do this he was reading books from Voltaire, Rousseau, John Locke, Montesquieu, and Machiavelli. He was memorizing the longest poems Edgar Allan Poe had to offer and would read articles in newspapers on microfilm from 1855 to about 1865 just to see what daily life was like. Ordinary folk singers in his time were not doing these things so it would then be no surprise when your audience regards you as extraordinary.

When it comes to art, the true reasons of the art live and die with the artist. We can interpret all we want, but we will never truly know. And as you can see in this case, Dylan didn't even know himself. He was a Titan in his time; the most commanding of all mythological creatures.

The Bigger Magic of Elizabeth Gilbert

Elizabeth Gilbert wrote a wonderful book, but it's not the one she is best known for. Eat, Pray, Love was fantastic, yes, but what we are going to discuss is her self-help book on creativity called Big Magic (8).

Back when the idea for this book was coming through me, it seemed everywhere I turned there were more and more signs pointing to help me derive a basis for what I call The Everspace. Big Magic is an example of that. Amazon sent me one of their trillion emails with the subject like, "Books recommended just for you!" I rolled my eyes, had my finger on the delete button and then something said, "Just check." As I opened the email there it was, marked down $9. I jumped on it without even reading the description. The sentiment, "sometimes the book just chooses you" rang loud and clear here.

In the book, Gilbert first talks about a man named Jack Gilbert (no relation), a wonderfully gifted poet who once again like Dylan lived in accordance to the laws of Nishkama Karma. Jack Gilbert's first collection of poems was published in 1962 and won several prestigious awards as well as winning over audiences and critics of all genres. Instead of taking the walk of fame he disappeared. He went and lived in Europe for 20 years, became largely forgotten and then published another book which people instantly loved as well. Again, Jack disappeared. When asked, he said he found his fame to be boring, and uninteresting. He was looking for a certain richness in life that could not be found through fame. Jack Gilbert was writing for writing's sake. He manifested what he needed to and left it for the world to decide. He didn't ask for anything in return, and in return life took care of him.

Towards the end of his life it seemed as though Gilbert had a need to pay it forward and took a position in the creative writing department at the University of Tennessee, Knoxville. When asked by his students what he was like, they said he was the most extraordinary man they have ever met, and, "didn't seem of this world." He told his students to write for the "delight" of it or out of "stubborn gladness."

How many of us take jobs for the delight of it, or because it makes you stubbornly glad? People will say that not everyone can be that lucky, but we are, and they are failing at lesson one already with a poor perspective. If you picked that up beforehand, good for you, you're learning. Now let's learn some more.

Ms. Gilbert then goes on to tell us about ideas. She says they arrive by inspiration; they work by manifesting themselves through a human partner (she says they are constantly swirling around us); and then we find out what happens when we say no. Once again we have another highly creative person claiming that ideas come from a sort of Ether. Call it the Universe, the Divine, The Everspace, the Ether. It's all relative, and it's real, but not until you believe it so.

In 2006, right after Gilbert published Eat, Pray, Love, she was sitting around wondering what she was going to do next. She was interested in writing a novel, but wasn't sure of the direction she wanted to take. Soon, an idea manifested based off of a story her sweetheart Felipe told her about when he was growing up in Brazil.

In the 1960's the Brazilian government got a wild idea to build a highway through the Amazon. Yes, the Amazon. It turns out that at the beginning construction was going fairly well, until well, the rainy season came. As it began to rain, as only it can rain in the Amazon, the crew found themselves trying to work in several feet of water. They had to disperse and come back when the rainy season was over. To their surprise, when they returned, the jungle slowly, but surely swallowed all that man had started to build. The road, equipment, and machines with tires as tall as a human were all buried. Nature wasn't having it.

This got Gilbert thinking of a murder-mystery-romance novel she called Evelyn of the Amazon and got to work on it right away. She started studying Portuguese, was calling experts, and purchased several books on Brazil. Then, right in the middle of writing her book, life happened and she got sidetracked for almost a year.

When she returned to writing, the idea was gone, and as hard as she tried, she just couldn't pick up where she left off. All of her notes, and research, and pages of this book she wrote were thrown in the trash. The manifestation of this book was finished, or was it?

Just around the time Gilbert realized this idea had gone away, she met another author named Ann Patchett in New York City at a panel discussion about libraries. She befriended Ann and they developed quite a relationship. After leaving New York, they actually became pen pals. Not through e-mail or social media; they wrote on real paper and sent the letters in real envelopes! Almost a year had passed before they had met face-to-face again for an event in Portland, Oregon. They met up for breakfast the morning of the event and starting telling each other about what they are working on next. To Gilbert's surprise, Ann starts talking about an Amazon jungle novel she is working on. Besides Ann's being contemporary, and Gilbert's being set in the 1960's, the storylines were almost EXACTLY the same. Gilbert was amazed. As they recounted when Gilbert lost the ability to manifest the idea, and Patchett received the idea to manifest it, it was right around the same time.

Funny thing is Gilbert had heard of ideas coming and going before when she talked to poet Ruth Stone. Stone grew up on a farm in Virginia and told Gilbert stories about when she was working the landscape and could actually "hear" a poem coming towards her like a stampede of buffalo. Stone said she would run like a crazy woman to her house and grab a pencil and a piece of paper so she could write down the poem as it passed through her. Where things really get interesting is when she would barely get there in time and she would literally grab the end of the poem as it was passing through her and she would have to write it on paper backwards! That's some seriously big magic there folks.

Stories like this are becoming more and more common. In Vishen Lakhiani's book: Code of the Extraordinary Mind (9) he talks about how Michael Jackson would wake up at 3 a.m. and call his manager saying he has to make a song right now or else Prince is going to do it. His manager thought he was acting ridiculous but it doesn't seem so now that we know what we know. While The Everspace may be easily accessible to others without even knowing it, for people like you and me it needs to be learned and

127

we need to start teaching that it can be TAUGHT. Talent is something we all have, but most of us don't know how to truly access it. The talent it takes to be extraordinary lies in having these selfless capabilities of Nishkama Karma. In order to get a clearer picture of this spiritual value, or way of thinking, we will analyze one more real-life story, which is probably the most shocking of all.

Found After Forty Years

"You put together two things that have not been put together before. And the world is changed. People may not notice at the time, but that doesn't matter. The world had been changed nonetheless."

-Julian Barnes, Levels of Life

Stephen Segerman and Craig Strydon grew up approximately 480km from each other in suburbs of South Africa. They both shared a calling that would wrap their fates together and eventually change one man's life along with theirs and several others forever.

In the 1970's and 1980's South Africa was still wrapped up in Apartheid, and even though Stephen was 10 years older than Craig, they both served in the South African Military due to this civil unrest. It was here that their destiny would be shaped even though they didn't serve at the same time, didn't even fire a bullet at the enemy, and exited the Army as fast as they possibly could. Rather than stress, adrenaline, or any of the other bonds that forge men of battle, Stephen and Craig would come together because of music.

Sixto Rodriguez was born in Detroit in 1942 and grew up the sixth son of two Mexican immigrant workers. Even though most of the civil rights cases were blacks against whites at that time, being brown was of really no benefit either and Sixto ended up being raised in a hotbed of race riots where a lot of tough things happened to a lot of tough people. Hard work was the only work these people knew. Sixto's Mother died when he was three, and it was now up to his older sister to step in and fill those shoes, since their dad was off working all day every day. When Sixto reached the age of 16 he signed up for the Army but for reasons undisclosed was rejected. It was at that time he picked up his first guitar and started playing.

Hank Williams, and Bob Dylan were big at that time. When they sang, they told stories, and as we heard already in the case of Dylan, people resonated with these stories very deeply. Rodriguez soon picked up on their vibe. By the age of 20 he was playing a bunch of small gig's around Detroit singing deep, meaningful songs that touched the hard-working class he lived amongst. Even with this talent, and a pretty good following, it wasn't enough to live on. With a wife, and their first child on the way Rodriguez was forced to earn more money, and ended up taking a job at one of Detroit's auto factories. While working one day, Rodriguez's attention must have wandered and he lost a finger on his left hand. As a right-handed guitarist, he had to use his left hand to finger the cords up top. This meant he had to teach himself how to play the guitar all over again.

After four more years of playing small gigs here and there Rodriguez's music caught the ear of Harry Balk who was the head of Impact Records and he ended up signing a deal to make music with him for five years. At 24 years of age, the young Rodriguez was well on his way to realizing his dreams as he laid 6 tracks down on his new album. In August of 1967 his first two singles were released, and got pretty good reviews. Impact released it under the name Rod Riguez because they thought his full name would have sounded too Hispanic and could hurt sales, and airtime. These were the delicate times people had to deal with then. Unfortunately for Rodriguez, Impact records ended up going out of business less than a year later, so he soon found himself jumping from club to club again until friends took some light recordings of his to a man named Clarence Avant, the owner of Sussex Records. Clarence loved his sound and agreed to produce his first full album.

After getting a band together and remixing some of his previous songs, the album was complete and released in March of 1970 with the title "Cold Fact." The entire band, and label felt like they just finished a Grammy winner. When the album hit the airwaves, the reviews coming in were extremely positive. The problem was that with little money to promote the album, the release of The Doors' Morrison Hotel, and Van Morrison's Moondance, Sixto's album got lost in the cracks like a gold coin in the couch. It was a total flop and Avant is quoted as saying literally only 6 copies were sold, mostly to family. Unbeknownst to anyone, Festival Records imported 400 copies into Australia, and A&M Records released Cold Fact on the Radio in 1971, both areas far, far away from its creator. Steve Rowland marches into his friend Freddy's office one day in the UK and notices something interesting on his desk. Freddy was heavily mixed up with Elvis at the time so he kind of knew what he was talking about when it came to music. It was the cover of Cold Fact that caught his eye and he asked Freddy if he could listen to it.

Freddy said sure, and off Steve went into the listening room. Within minutes he became incredibly excited by what he was listening to. He marched back into Freddy's office and said if Sixto is going to make a second album, he wants produce it. Avant got wind of this and since it was a pretty epic time for anyone to be recording in London, he pulled the plug at Sussex and sent Rodriguez overseas.

With 10 new songs already written by Rodriguez, recording started the day after he arrived and everyone working with him was excited. It is rumored that they finished the album in three weeks, which is lightning fast in the music business. Sixto's second album Coming From Reality was released in November of 1971 to rave reviews. As Rodriguez and his crew sat back and waited for it to take off, they were met again only with confusion. The album wasn't selling. In December of 1971 Sussex Records dropped Sixto from his contract, and in July of 1975, Sussex itself folded into oblivion.

With his music career seemingly over, Sixto went back to working construction in Detroit. Juggling work, a family, and a couple small gigs here and there, he figured that if he can't make a difference with his music, he would do it through politics. He got involved with various Chicano and grassroots organizations, as well as some Native American pow-wows. Rodriguez would run for office 8 times as well, losing every single time. This guy couldn't catch a break and when people asked him why he did such backbreaking labor or why he wanted to make a difference his only answer was "It keeps the blood circulating." Most people would have given up, been complaining up a storm, or turned to drugs to numb what most consider to be failure, but to those closest to him

Rodriguez was a staunch advocator of never looking back, and only pressing forward. He was not one to ask what's in it for him; he was doing what he was doing to help others (The amazing thing was that with all of this going on Rodriguez also managed to get his PhD from Wayne State University's Monteith College in 1981).

Even with these new endeavors, Rodriguez never stopped playing music. His wife said he would roam from room to room everyday looking for the best sounding acoustics, or sometimes he would lock himself in a single room and play for hours. He was also a fixture at the main Detroit library, which was within walking distance from his home. A lover of Philosophy, he read all he could on the subject. Nearing 40 years of age Rodriguez just accepted his path in life. Artists are told that if you don't make it by the time you're 30, chances are slim to none you ever will. With life normalizing, Rodriguez would get a phone call one day in 1979 that may just make him part of the slim to none category.

One fateful day in 1979, Sixto Rodriguez received a call from a tour promoter in Australia. Rodriguez was informed that his albums have been flying off the shelves and they wanted to know if he would be willing to set up some tour dates. What's amazing is Rodriguez never asked where all of his royalties are for the sold albums. He doesn't start hiring 16 attorneys and start suing everyone.

Overwhelmed, and humbled, Rodriguez simply agreed to the tour and off he went with his wife and two children down under. While touring, people noticed how he was almost embarrassed to be on stage with so many people idolizing him. In an article published by Rolling Stone magazine, when Rodriguez was once asked to go onstage for an encore and say something to the fans he could only manage to squeak out, "Eight years later, and this happens. I don't believe it (10)". With the tour being incredibly successful, the promoters brought him back for a second one in 1981. Again, playing to sold out shows Rodriguez could not believe the fame he acquired through these songs he all but forgotten about. After returning to the USA from his second sold out Australian tour, Rodriguez was hoping someone in the States was going to hear about his fame in Australia but nothing ever came about. The phones never rang. In classic Rodriguez style, he went right back to what he knew best, which was sweeping out homes and digging dirt on construction sites.

In mid-1997, while Sixto Rodriguez was still earning a paycheck through construction, Steve Segerman, and Craig Strydon were sitting in a coffee shop in Cape Town, South Africa in comparing notes. They met each other through e-mail and also found out they shared a similar passion for finding the artist known as Sixto Rodriguez. To them, Sixto was a legend, but he was also a ghost. They had both became enchanted by Rodriguez's music when they were in the army as Cold Fact (Rodriguez's first album) was somewhat of an Army anthem and would frequently be played over the loud speakers in the morning. Naturally, when an artist inspires you, you want to learn more about them. As both of these men went digging for answers they couldn't find anything. The Internet was too young so information on Sussex Records was nonexistent, and what was even worse was there were rumors floating around that Rodriguez was dead by his own hand.

The answers were different every time someone mentioned it. "He shot himself on stage after reciting his own epitaph." "He died in a fire when his electric guitar malfunctioned." Or my personal favorite, "He set himself on fire on stage at one of his concerts." This was not just South African people making up crazy lies. In Australia they believed Rodriguez died of a heroin overdose in a New York City gutter. How these rumors started nobody knows, but Rodriguez's legendary status in South Africa because of them is comparable to how people became much more interested in The Doors when Jim Morrison died. Steve and Craig spoke for about an hour that day but ended up leaving with the same questions. Is Rodriguez alive? If so, where is he? If not, how did he die? Steve figured rather than them looking for information, they should have the information come to them so he created a website asking people with information on Sixto Rodriguez to come forward. One day, Rodriguez's daughter just happened to stumble on to the website and ended up sending an e-mail to Steve letting him know that her father is alive and well. Steve informed her of how big he is in South Africa and once again they had no idea. She said Rodriguez has not seen a dime in royalties from his music that has sold in South Africa and Steve was shocked. Steve gave his phone number to her and asked if she would have Rodriguez call him. She said she would, but that her father was a private man and she couldn't guarantee anything. To Steve's surprise he got a late-night call that same day from the man himself.

Even though his voice was unmistakable, Steve couldn't believe that he was talking to the man whose records (and whereabouts) he had been obsessing over for nearly 20 years. Once again Rodriguez didn't ask about royalties or any money he was owed, he was simply overjoyed to hear that his music was appreciated by so many. The humility of Rodriguez, more importantly the Nishkama Karma spirit this man has shines through on so many levels. In the book Sugar Man: The Life, Death, and Resurrection of Sixto Rodriguez (11), there are multiple accounts of people talking about his hard work ethic, his generosity, and his selfless nature. A few recognizable quotes are:

"(On touring) How sweet they are to even notice me because there's so much music out there, and that they made that happen, I owe them so much, man."

"(On him as a performer) What I do as a performer. I let the guitar win them over. I accept my craft and I give it back to them, and they recognize it."

"(On his lack of fame in America until now) "I was too disappointed to be disappointed, besides, nothing beats reality."

Vivekananda says we are entitled to our work, but not the fruits thereof. Sixto Rodriguez has been a shining example of this statement as you can see even from the previous three quotes.

Once the people of South Africa got ahold of Sixto Rodriguez they would not let him go. He has done several tours there, drawing bigger and bigger crowds each time. An amusing part of the story is that the tour promoters actually had to convince people Rodriguez was alive and that they were not just going to see a look-alike. Once he got onstage for the first time the voice was unmistakable and people knew it was really him. A few years went by and a record company called Light in the Attic based out of Seattle, Washington acquired the rights to Rodriguez's music and re-released both albums in 2008, and 2009 respectively. Both albums were positively reviewed and after nearly 40 years, Rodriguez finally had his recognition among the American people. In 2012, a documentary about his life entitled "Searching for Sugarman" won an Oscar and that set the stage for talk show appearances galore among other gigs. He was asleep when the announcement came that the documentary had won and is the first to admit he only appears in the film for 8 minutes. If his music is for the people, then his movie is too.

Sixto Rodriguez had every reason in the world to be a bitter man. Some artists are bitter or head down a road of self-destruction even though they can get their talents to the masses. Fame, or lack of fame is kind of like tasting ice cream for the first time. Ice cream is what we call hyper-palatable food. Your brain sends your hormones into overdrive because fat, sugar, and salt do not occur together anywhere in nature. Now imagine you just had a bite, and your body is going nuts from the taste. You can't control the cravings you just want more. This is your brain on fame. Now imagine you can see on TV or hear people on the radio talking about how good ice cream is but you can't have any. This is your brain on not achieving fame. That will drive someone crazy too. Nishkama Karma teaches us to work hard so other people can have your ice cream. Crazy, right?

I don't think Sixto Rodriguez would agree with you.

Your Key to Accessing The Everspace:

Non-Attachment & Abundance VS Scarcity

One of the most difficult concepts for human beings in developed countries to grasp is the idea of non-attachment. We think because we bought something, or because something has our name on it, that it is ours; that we OWN it and nobody has a right to it but us. Some people take this concept so far that they think they can actually "own" another person, and I'm not just talking about slavery. From a legal standpoint, you may own an object, but The Ever Space, as you can see, does not care about ownership. What it manifests is for everyone to enjoy.

In order to fully access this space to have abundance given to us, we must believe in abundance first. Some people have a scarcity belief in life, that there is not enough to go around so you need as much as you can, and if you lose any of it you're screwed. This limits your thinking and always put you on the defensive. You become dualistic (which we will talk about in the next lesson) and now have to protect everything you own. Now this isn't saying that you can't own nice things, it's simply saying that like your body, everything on this planet is only rented to us, we never truly "OWN" anything. You come in with nothing and you leave with nothing. You can make money, have nice houses, and marry the prettiest girl in the world, but just remember that none of it belongs to you.

Many people lose a job and feel their life is over. Other people lose a boyfriend, girlfriend, or get divorced and swear they will never love again, but you will. Negative lessons in life teach, positive lessons in life reward. Which would you rather have more of? How do you expect to grow in your life if you do not learn from the negatives? Your girlfriend wants to go out with her friends for the fourth night in a row? Let her and be happy. That's not YOUR girl. She is not an object and does not belong to you. Someone at work took your idea and now looks better in front of the boss? Good for them, the true beneficiary is going to go to the needs of someone else, stop worrying about your own. These are tough, tough concepts that take time to learn and implement but pay off big when it comes to your mental health and well-being. Having a mind clear of regrets, and resentment brings you into a more present state and in turn closer to what you truly desire.

Uncomfortability Challenge

Every once in a while, when you have the time or the mood strikes you, do something for someone, or a group of people, without letting them know, and without taking credit for it. Work at a soup kitchen for an afternoon without telling anybody where you were or making it your Facebook status update. Give the cashier at a random coffee shop $50 and tell him/her to pay for the next 10 customers or until the money is used up. Don't leave a name, and don't tweet about it. You can even just put the money in an envelope and just hand it to someone behind the counter. If they keep it, then that's on them, and we don't mind because THAT'S NOT OUR MONEY ANYWAY! You can wash someone's car when they're not home, or leave a gift basket on a neighbor's doorstep early in the morning. You can even leave a movie card on the desk of a coworker you have difficulty getting along with. You may even include a note admiring them for a job well done. The possibilities are endless, but hopefully these few got your gears moving.

References:
1. Help Others, But Don't Expect Gratitude in Return | Nishkama Karma of the Gita. (n.d.). Retrieved November 16, 2016, from http://www.spiritualbee.com/posts/nishkama-karma-bhagavad-gita/
2. Vivekananda, S. (2015). Karma Yoga: The Yoga of Action (Art of Living) [EditionNEXT.com].
3. Brown, M. (Director). (2015). The Man Who Knew Infinity [Motion picture on Amazon Videos]. UK: Animus Films.
4. McRaney, D. (2011). You are not so smart: Why you have too many friends on Facebook, why your memory is mostly fiction, and 46 other ways you're deluding yourself. New York: Gotham Books/Penguin Group.
5. Dylan, B. (2004). Chronicles: Volume one. New York: Simon & Schuster.
6. Lehrer, J. (2012). The neuroscience of Bob Dylan's genius. Retrieved November 16, 2016, from https://www.theguardian.com/music/2012/apr/06/neuroscience-bob-dylan-genius-creativity (I realize Leher lied about quoting Dylan in this article and his book on creativity, but I used it for the science, and the science still stands).
7. Bob Dylan: Songs were "almost magically written" (n.d.). Retrieved November 16, 2016, from http://top.adlesse.com/en/i/871353166015052722/bob-dylan-songs-were-almost-magically-written
8. Gilbert, E. (2015). Big magic: Creative living beyond

fear. New York: Riverhead Books.

9. Lakhiani, V. (2016). The code of the extraordinary mind: Ten unconventional laws to redefine your life & succeed on your own terms. Emmaus, PA: Rodale.

10. Greene, A. (n.d.). Rodriguez: 10 Things   You Don't Know About the 'Searching for Sugar Man' Star. Retrieved November 16, 2016, from http://www.rollingstone.com/music/news/rodriguez-10-things-you-dont-know-about-the-searching-for-sugar-man-star-20130328

EverLesson 5: Control Your Ego

"One may understand the cosmos, but never the ego. The self is more distant than any star."

-G. K. Chesterton

"What other people think of me is none of my business. One of the highest places you can get to is being independent of the good opinions of other people."

-Dr. Wayne Dyer

You Can Practice, but You Can't Play

When Bill Walton was coming out of high school he was being heralded as the best player in college basketball before he even set foot on the court. Standing 7-feet tall, he was smart, athletic, and had a passion for the game already at a very young age. Combine this with playing for the best coach in college basketball, John Wooden at UCLA, and you had a very potent mixture.
Bill Walton's career reads like an evil wife's grocery list. Here is a condensed version (1):

* 2x NBA Champion (1977, 1986)
* NBA Finals MVP (1977)
* NBA MVP (1978)
* 2 Time NBA All-Star (1977, 1978)
* 2x NBA All-Defensive First Team (1977, 1978)
* NBA Rebounding leader (1977)
* NBA Blocks Leader (1977)
* His Number was retired by the Portland Trailblazers
* 2x NCAA Champion (1972, 1973)
* 2x NCAA Final Four Most Outstanding Player (1972, 1973)
* 3x National College Player of the Year (1972-1974)
* His Number Retired by UCLA
* He is in the NBA Hall of Fame
* He is in the College Basketball Hall of Fame

While Walton had a great professional career, he was all but unstoppable in his college days. As a junior, he single handedly won his second straight national title by scoring 21 of 22 shots from the field, beating Memphis State 87-

66. That's right, he scored 44 points, and the rest of his team scored 43.

Poised to be the first player taken in the NBA draft in 1974, reporters were asking Walton whom the best player was that he played against in his college career. Without hesitation, he pointed down to the end of the court and said, "That guy down there is the best player I have ever played against. Swen Nater."

Who?

Swen Nater's parents divorced when he was 3 years old. She would remarry, but soon the family fell on hard times and they decided to move to America in search of a new beginning. Swen's mother was forced to put him, and his younger sister in an orphanage before she left taking only Swen's baby brother with her. After a couple of years, a TV show caught wind of the occurrence and reunited Swen and his sister with his Mom in America. Swen was now 9 years old living in America and didn't speak a single word of English.

By the time Swen was a junior in high school, he was 6'11" tall. Many people were telling him he should go play basketball, but the problem was that his motor skills didn't catch up to his long, lanky body. Simply put, he looked like Gumby out on the court. He tried out his senior year and made the team, but when he graduated from high school he went on to work as a mechanic rather than go to college like most of his friends.

One day the local community college basketball coach was getting his car fixed and he notice that the guy working on his car had his feet sticking out of one end and his head out of the other. By now, Swen's body had matured and with a little convincing he went to play basketball for Cypress Community College. Within 2 years he was one of the best junior college basketball players in the country and the offers to play division one started rolling in. His coach however, had connections with John Wooden, the coach over at UCLA. He convinced Coach Wooden to sign Swen to his last remaining scholarship spot by using logic. The logic he used was that Bill Walton was coming in as a highly-publicized freshman at 7 feet tall. Their next tallest player was 6'9" and Swen was 6'11". Walton needed someone of his stature to compete with and that's why Wooden gave in. Before giving in, he sat Swen down and said this, "I'm going to make you two promises, One, you'll probably never ever get off the bench. But two, you're going to get a chance every day to practice against the best player in America, and I promise you, the best coaches in America are going to work with you every day (2)."

Swen Nater agreed and went on to become the first person ever in the history of the NBA to be drafted without starting a single college game in his career.

How many of us would have had the poise, and control of their ego the way Swen Nater did at such a young age to make the choice that he did? Most of us would say, "Sorry Coach Wooden, but I'm in this to play and be a star, I'm nobody's practice dummy." Nater had offers from other Universities; teams in the ABA were already drafting him as well. He could have gone somewhere else and been THE MAN. But he chose to go to UCLA and be the man behind the man. He chose to help someone else get better and in the process he became better himself.

Today, Swen Nater is the Vice President of Costco, and he wrote a book titled, "You haven't Taught Until They Have Learned." Which is based off of the principles he learned from Coach Wooden. For every Swen Nater out there, there are probably a couple hundred thousand who are his opposite. Some might say this is what is wrong with the world, but they are wrong. Ego may be the antithesis of good sometimes, but because most of us cannot totally destroy it, our only hope comes in recognizing and controlling it. It's thinking before you speak. Acting rather than reacting. It's knowing that no matter how much someone takes away from you, you will not be diminished the way modern society thinks.

Guarding the Gates of Hell

"Your own self-realization is the greatest service you can render upon the world."

-Ramana Maharshi

Cerberus, in Greek Mythology is a three-headed dog that guards the gates of hell. Like Cerberus, I believe our egos have three heads as well, guarding who you perceive you are. They are:

1. The Body
2. The Thinker (Or the imaginator)
3. The Resistor

All three of these ugly heads combine to mess up our lives through our day-to-day activities. We become convinced that the way we are acting is for our greater good, yet when we measure where we are against where we want to be, we always fall short. Something is always missing, we are never satisfied, and we turn a beautiful existence into a living hell. We wake up tired, we go to school or work in a bad mood, we kick the dog when we come home, and we go to bed in a drunken stupor to forget it all.

The first step is acknowledging you have one. I have one, the Pope has one, and Richard Nixon definitely had one. The key though is work. The ego is deceptive. Beat it one day, and it will trick you the next. Just when you feel comfortable and think that you have the hang of it, BOOM, something happens that sends you in a tailspin like you never saw it coming. The ego has been written about for as long as man could put pen to paper, but still there is no course that teaches about it in any school. It's as if it is something you should just figure out on your own. For most of us, by the time we realize we are in the grips of ego, it is too late. Ego, in any form, as I'm sure you have figured out by now, will not be admitted into The Everspace. If you are living according to the laws of Nishkama Karma, ego is already being dealt a mortal blow, but there are other considerations we still have to be made aware of.

The Body

When you look at your body, naked, in front of a mirror what do you see? Imperfections? Maybe you work out really hard and you see perfection. Whatever the case, any image you project on how you look, or how you should look, comes from your ego and it's all complete bullshit. I should look like this, there shouldn't be any fat there, or my nose looks German and I hate it. This is where the ego of our body manifests. It is constantly unhappy with

146

what it sees and demands change. When we do make a change, it wants another change, and so on. The list never stops. It's what makes people have plastic surgery 32 times just to get it right, and even then, they still aren't happy. Our greatest gift in life is being unique. One of a kind. Our body was given to us as a manifestation of the Beloved and being content with our image is the first step to defeating the ego. Now this doesn't mean we should never work out, or lose weight, those are healthy aspects that contribute to a longer happier lifestyle. Obsessing over short stature, or small breasts and feeling dislike for who you are and what you look like takes you on the fast track to nowhere.

The Everspace is all about love and acceptance. If you don't love and accept your physical body, how can you manifest love and acceptance towards others? You make it that much harder for your boyfriend, girlfriend, or spouse to love you when you are constantly complaining about yourself. Your obsession becomes your own downfall. People will get sick and tired of hearing how unhappy you are with your larger than normal ears that they will start to distance themselves from you. It works in other ways too. Saying my knee hurts or my back hurts are normally excuses to keep us comfortable. The ego is all about self-preservation. It wants to make sure it looks the best, always wins, or is the most admired in any situation. If you think you are going to get beat in a footrace, or weightlifting competition, your ego will make excuses as to why you lost, or why you are not going to compete in the first place. It's a rejecter of the present. A destroyer of the truth. And it will go through many different measures to stay intact.

The ego can be defined as a dysfunction with any current

moment. The word person comes from the Latin word "persona", which means, "character in a drama, mask." Every day, each one of us puts on our best mask to show the world we are worthy of their attention. If we get a pimple on prom night, we curl up into a little ball and hide. Surely that's never happened to a prepubescent male or female before. We see ourselves as separated from everyone else and start to wish for something other than what our life is right now. No amount of crying, or makeup can hide reality though, but that doesn't stop us from trying. I said earlier, that the ego is always going to be responsible for the preservation of the self. Nowhere is this more evident than when we associate our self with material things. How many times have you looked at something on the rack in a store and went to try it on only to look in the mirror and say, "Oh this doesn't look like me at all!" Now it's true that we all have our own style, it's what makes us unique, but to be that strongly associated with material things is a very egoic controlling mechanism.

Manufacturers know this and market specifically to our own sense of self and especially to our egos. Look at all the Tapout gear people walk around in. You think all of these guys walk around fighting people or tapping them out? No way. But that is a front they want to put on. Look at my shirt, I'm tough because tough guys on TV wear the same shirt as I do. Beat it buddy! You can look at the Champs Sports "we know game" commercials that came out in 2012. There is an invisible boy walking on the street as articles of clothing magically appear on him. The voice over says, "This isn't just your shoe, it's your first step, this isn't just your tee shirt, it's your message, and this isn't just your hat, it's your crown." Manufacturers are trying to get you to identify "things" with "being," and the only way they can do that is by placing meaning on their products and have you associate with that. Sadly, we invent, or buy things just to impress each other. There is no spiritual or deeper meaning behind that new watch, it is just a status symbol you can wear on your wrist saying, "Look everybody! I made it!" It takes a bold person to stand up in front of others with imperfections and not be swayed by the whispers, or looks of dissent. It takes confidence, yet we don't realize confidence is not, "they will like me with my imperfections." Confidence is "I will be fine if they don't like me with my imperfections." It's a self-love that nobody can take away from you in any situation. It takes an inner strength in realizing you are not your body, that your body is simply a vessel for you to do work in this world. Look at Nick Vujicic, the man was born without arms or legs and makes a living touring the world inspiring others! Nick says, "If God can use a man without arms and legs to be His hands and feet, then He will certainly use any willing heart! (3)."

I've seen old cars, old buildings, or dusty old streets that I prefer much more to the modern ones. Does a deformed tree, or a stagnant muddy pond, care about its features so much to hide from others? Does a mountain look out over the valley and say those mounds of dirt and rock look better than me? Does a pigeon with one foot, or a dog with three legs lie around and feel sorry for itself? The answer is unequivocally no. Nothing in life but human beings are unhappy with the way they look, how they feel, or what they have. A fish will freeze in an artic pond without ever feeling sorry for itself. A dog will still look for the affection of the owner that beats it. To combat this, we must practice acceptance. Acceptance doesn't mean we lie down and just wait to die. Acceptance means that we are at peace with our body at all times and any way it looks. We have many different bodies in our lifetime and we must accept them all. Look at your body when you were one year old, now compare it to your four-year-old body. Compare your four-year-old body to your ten-year-old body and so on. When did you become uncomfortable with what you look like? Go back to that time and figure out what is bothering you and then come to terms with accepting it. If you can't accept it, then accept that you can't accept it. If you can't do that then find a middle ground between accepting what you can and working on what you can't. The underlying tone here is work. Most of us go to work in our lives but do not work ON our lives and this is where we fail. Let me buy different clothes, or more makeup to hide what I do not like about myself, because I have no idea how to improve myself or accept what I do not like. This is because for most of us the way we are taught to think about our body's image is totally incorrect.

Kanye Watts

If I were to ask you to name one talented artist you feel has a pretty big ego, most of us would say Kanye West. In a recent concert in Sacramento, California, West showed up a half-hour late, played two songs, and then went on a rant for 10 minutes about Beyoncé, Donald Trump, and how he is going to run for president in 2020 (4). West then dropped the microphone and walked off stage. Mr. West's musical talents are unrivaled. Some may say he is one of the best rappers alive today, and with 21 million records, plus 66 million digital downloads sold, they wouldn't be too far off the mark. What is off the mark is the fact that instead of paying to listen to someone else's ego, there is a man who is willing to help you learn how to control your ego for free.

Alan Watts was a British philosopher that helped Western cultures understand Eastern philosophical principles through countless lecturing, and his writings of 28 books on the various subjects. To give you an understanding of how well this man is hidden, he has 370,000 likes on his Facebook page, while Kanye has 9.4 million. Watts is teaching you to live better and control your ego, and West is teaching you how to act outlandish and for self-interest. Interesting, no? But I digress.

In one of Watts' lectures, he opens up with the statement, "I wonder what you mean when you use the word "I." He contends that most of us have no idea, and those that do have a false sense of personal identity, which leads us around like a dog chasing its tail. As a result, we grow up believing that we are separate from nature and that nature is a force that must conquered or at least controlled. In doing this we put our self at odds with nature, and rather than flowing with it like water does down a river, we become resistant to everything life provides for us.

Most of us believe that we came into this world, but Watts argues that we came OUT of this world, the way a flower comes out of the soil, or the apple in a tree. In other words, we do not live in nature, we ARE nature, and nature does not make mistakes. Your red hair, your freckles, your short stature is all to be loved and accepted, because by not accepting it, it equates to not accepting life because you are an expression of life. Most of us will agree that all life is intelligent. Nobody is telling trees, or grass to grow, just like fish don't have to remind themselves to eat. They are all led by this common intelligence life provides for us. Human beings have this intelligence inside of us as well, but most of us are walking around not happy with what we have, trying to change what we don't like, so this common intelligence becomes buried. Lost. And when spiritual teachers talk about enlightenment, or when I'm trying to communicate this felling of The Everspace, you roll your eyes, put your headphones on, and turn Kanye up.

Deny your gifts and no further gifts will be given. But if you accept what you have, and what you look like, and express gratitude for it, the song of life will come back singing for you once again. Think about it. Right at this very moment your body is pushing five liters of blood through miles of vessels, and miles of nerves are sensing trillions of cells undergoing millions of chemical reactions. You're not "doing" any of this, it is being done for you. At the same time, we must realize that if we take away those five liters of blood, you die. If we take away one breath, you pass out. Pain to me, is always a reminder of just how fragile life can be. Pain for all of us should be a reminder that life is showing us how to survive, but most of us walk around in pain every day, complaining about it. That's the ego. Poor me. Why me? I don't deserve this. Deny your ego the pleasure of thinking you are your body because you are not. Your body is a vessel and must be loved, respected, and taken care of in order for you to do the work you were born to do.

So, back to the statement of what we mean when we use the word "I." In a talk entitled What Is, Watts describes how the thinking mind reduces the world to words, numbers, and symbols, which creates a problem because you cannot quench someone's thirst by saying the word water, or you can't eat a dollar bill and derive nutrition out of it. We become people that confuse the world and what it is, with a world that is talked about and figured about. He says it's like going out and eating menus instead of dinners, which in turn leaves us psychologically frustrated. The term "I" he says is what we consider the symbol of ourselves, and rather than just being a physical body, should include the whole psychophysical organism, conscious, and unconscious, PLUS its environment. Your real self is the Universe centered on your organism (5). When we have an egotistical view of our body, we are not centered. We are aligning our "self" with an imaginary extreme. We are asking the matter of our body to become bigger, smaller, or something else entirely, which kicks us out of the flow of the Universe.

When it comes to entering The Everspace, you must give up the ego's view of your body. That doesn't mean you can't improve it through the use of quality foods, and exercise; your body is the greatest tool you will ever have, use it! What it means is to stop chasing an alternate version of yourself. Stop wishing for more than you have been given. Stop thinking your body is separate from nature or the Universe. Even saying we are all one is incorrect. The Hindu's say "Non-Dual," which is interpreted as "Not Two." Practice self-love and tenderness with your judgments and you will cultivate a space of peace and acceptance through which the Universe can once again work through you.

The Thinker (Or the Imaginator)

"Anytime there is a struggle between doing what is actually right, and what seems right, then your ego is interfering with your decision."

-Darren L. Johnson

Understanding our sense of self helps us to reconnect with life. To do this we already learned how to not let the ego lead you into the trap of thinking you "are" your body. But what about your mind? We all walk around on a day-to-day basis with verbal banter running rampant in our minds, of which scientists say 80% is repetitive. What I'm going to say to you may come as a shock, but I want you to get rid of that voice. Divorce it. Uncreate and delete it. Unfriend it. While this may be easier said than done, we can use a real-world example as to why we should. Imagine a friend of yours came over to spend the day with you. Throughout the entire day, 8 out of 10 sentences were the same, and let's say those 8 sentences are criticisms of you or other people. Not so bad? OK, what about if those sentences were about how great he or she was in relation to you? That's pretty irritating, but still, maybe you could hack it. OK, what about if those sentences were complaints? How long would you be able to hang out with this person? Now imagine seeing them every single day no matter what. How long would it take you to never want to see or hear from this person again? A week? Maybe two, till you stopped returning their calls and avoided them like the plague? What's amazing is we all live with a version of this person every day. We have made it our best friend and we believe everything it says.

My life turned around when I started to question my thoughts. Why am I thinking this? Where did that come from? That's a really odd conclusion Chris, how did you figure that? Like I said in the beginning of the book, my inner voice was relentless. Rather than beat myself up and create more stress, all I did was stop believing EVERYTHING and started to pick and choose which thoughts I took advantage of. The old saying goes, "The only way to settle muddy water is by leaving it alone." I

154

separated my thinking mind from my intuitive mind, and after some time, slowly but surely, a calming stillness came over me and I started to hear things more clearly. Even the voice in my head changed its tune from positive to negative.

The ego is smart though. It will play your game, love everybody, and if you're not being careful it will start to insert its own agenda when you least expect it and all of a sudden you catch yourself being angry about the past, or having anxiety about the future. Expect to play this game for the rest of your life.

The biggest lesson, no, the greatest trick the ego pulls, is to make you believe that just because you "think" something, that it is actually true. The ego is always going to give reasons to support its position and will easily fool you. When we associate the voice in our head with cold, hard truth, we are being tricked by the ego and its ultimate interest, which rarely includes what is absolutely true.

Your brain is a living processor and needs content. It does not matter what content, anything will do. The problem with today's world is that most of the content is negative, and the thinking brain will take that negative information and turn it into a story. This story is going to be limited by your past experiences, as well as your own creativity. This creates chaos when mixed with our emotions and can quickly send us spinning out of control, causing us to imagine circumstances or solutions that just aren't there. In Ryan Holiday's book, Ego Is The Enemy (6) we learn how John DeLorean left a great job at GM to produce his own line of futuristic-looking cars The man was a genius and felt that he could run his own car company better, but this was his ego talking and over time proved to be irrational. Soon, DeLorean and his company spun out of control and lost his investors millions of dollars. I don't care how much you love Back to the Future, if you research his story you'll learn the manufacturing process of the car was a disaster from start to finish. Delorean's last stand was to smuggle in $60 million dollars' worth of cocaine with the cash he had left. He was caught by the cops, and despite videotape of him giddy, holding up a bag of cocaine saying, "This stuff is as good as gold", he was acquitted due to entrapment. Some of you may be saying, "but he got off", while I say, what is a car manufacturer doing with $60 million dollars in cocaine in the first place! There's just no reason to go there, but with the ego, where there's a will there's a way. Because our imagination is so powerful, it overpowers our intelligence. It wants the next thing, and the next thing after that, and the next thing after that, with absolutely no plan on how to acquire any of it until you find out you've gone from car god to drug lord overnight.

Holiday also discusses the demise of John Kennedy Toole. Toole wrote the book *A Confederacy of Dunces* that was rejected by every publisher he sent it to. Toole was so distraught that he committed suicide in his car on an empty road in Biloxi, Mississippi. After his death, his mother found a carbon copy of the manuscript and kept submitting it on his behalf until it was finally accepted. It won the Pulitzer Prize in 1981 for fiction. This is the power of the thinking mind. It can create hope when there is none in the case of John DeLorean, or it can create despair when there is hope in the case of John Kennedy Toole.

The thinking mind needs labels to exist. It needs to know you are somebody, going somewhere, doing something.

156

Without labels, the mind and therefore the ego have nothing to grasp. You will find it working overtime when you are bored and have nothing to do. You'll sit and think about all the people who wronged you, or how that one person you loved got away. You'll think about how if you had more money you'd finally be happy living the life of your dreams. You'll think about how your friend Melissa needs to lose a few pounds, or how irritating your brother is because he listens to music too loud in the evening. All of this is meant to be a trap. What do traps do? They don't let you progress, they don't let you move forward in life. Traps are designed to keep you right where you are. The labels are there to keep you comfortable and make you feel as though you are right about everything. You don't have to do any work because you know everything already. You don't have to live life to experience anything because you've already read about that in a magazine somewhere.

In the book, Aleph, by Paulo Coelho, he says, "People want to make the excuse that they don't have enough money to travel, but it's not money you need to travel, it's courage (7)." Going to a different country can be downright scary and casts you well out of your comfort zone, which your ego doesn't like. People may have many different reasons to travel, I fully advocate it, but I believe Mark Twain said it best when he said, "Travel is fatal to racism (and concurrently your ego)." James Altucher advocates buying experiences over buying things because experiences add layers to our life. We learn about the world and we learn about ourselves, which in return makes us more cultured and aware.

In a podcast by Ram Dass called "The Thinking Mind (8)", he exposes our thought patterns when it comes to ego and gives us solutions to defeat it. He describes how in the West we admire intellect over wisdom and gives the example of politics, which is pretty relevant today considering the circus act we were all witnesses to for the 2016 presidential election. You can't be stupid to get where Donald Trump or Hilary Clinton have gotten. There's a certain knowledge that comes with getting to where they have gotten, but you don't sense there's a lot of wisdom. This is because wisdom cannot be learned in a textbook. Wisdom comes from having the courage to learn from mistakes you have made through your life's experience. It has a certain innocence to it that transcends truth the thinking mind can grasp and ends up turning into something we can feel. You can't feel knowledge; all you can do is appreciate it.

People who have wisdom will say, "I've done it this way and I was wrong." People with knowledge only want to proclaim how right they are, but you are not going to get where you want to through righteousness. If you think you're smart because you're always right, that is the egoic trap. The greatest successes have come through failure after failure and taking chances. By not taking calculated risks, the ego has something to protect. It hoards to keep you safe and through this mechanism you may be able to sustain life, but you will never be truly happy because this way of thinking creates resentment and nobody will be truly happy wishing they had done something different in the past.

The thinking mind is great for a lot of things, but we need to realize it is not the only game in town. What most of us lack is the ability to use our intuition. Connecting with our intuitive self is the key to understanding and living your life's purpose. All we have to do Ram Dass says is, "change the relative power positions of the two," listening to our intuition first, and our thinking mind second. We can use the mind to set up a schedule, drive a car, go grocery shopping, or plan a party with friends, but for life-altering decisions we must primarily use our intuition with a little bit of the thinking mind. For example, a friend of mine just switched jobs based on what her intuition was telling her. She worked in her family business for 14 years and towards the end of her tenure came to several realizations that no longer supported her to continue working there. In a matter of 3 months she made a gut decision to change and it was the right one. Before the switch there was a little bit of fear, and a little bit of anxiety, but after the switch she was filled with jubilation on her newfound freedom and creative control she was given at her new job.

Now there's a lot going on there. Leaving the family business? Based off of intuition? Most people would have taken the position that family comes first, or never bite the hand that feeds you. Most people would have defended their position to stay content and not grow. Eckhart Tolle says, "Know that when you become defensive about something, you have identified yourself with an illusion." This wasn't a selfish move, or done in spite of anyone. She resigned with the utmost love and respect for everything that was afforded her. Ego would have kept her in the trap, but being able to control her ego helped her move forward. This would have also opened the door for the imagination, worrying about every negative thing 50 miles down the road. Your brain starts to create fictitious scenarios based off of no solid proof or information, leaving you again afraid of your own shadow, unable to move. What about this, or what about that? Our mind races, and then fear kicks in.

Our intuition has 2 parts to it. We have our intuitive mind, and our intuitive heart. Your intuitive heart is the master and is there to lead you. Like we saw from the evidence that HeartMath provided, the heart gets the signal first and sends it to the brain. Your intuitive mind then is there to direct you through the steps necessary in order to achieve your goals. This is a system of checks and balances, which provides insight on several different levels. Your intuitive mind isn't just thought; it is thought combined with feeling. This requires a lot of self-reflection and the ego doesn't like that because it wants to be the master, not the servant.

Thinking is a power that we have, but we cannot get lost in that power because it is only one way of knowing the world. The thinking mind only thinks about things or objects, which makes it difficult to grasp anything that is intangible. If I can't see it, touch it, or smell it, then I don't believe in it. This once again shuts off our ability to hear life's cues through our intuition. The thinking mind isolates us and keeps reinforcing your own sense of separateness which cuts you off from The Everspace and then you sit around confused wondering why you're all alone. You're alone because that's the signal you were sending. Me, me, me, me, me. Where did everybody go? Thinking makes you believe you have control over something but control is an illusion because it's made up. It's a word we use to describe a hypothetical situation. It's the same as power. You don't have power; you have somebody else's sense of the illusion of power. And that's the thinking ego's game, illusion. No matter how much you "think", you will never achieve a sense of contentment, or oneness, or wholeness. It will always be you against the world.
We have all gone through a certain point in our life where we start to think we are not who we think we are. There

are times where we surprise even ourselves and look back in disbelief. That was the door to your prison. It was flung open for a quick second, left unguarded, and like a caged bird you stood and just stared at it, regressing back to what you think you know. Often times the cosmos will come to us in the form of dreams, déjà vu, or hallucinations, but we use excuses or discover some scientific article that helps bring us back down to reality. The problem we have as human beings isn't our limitations; it's our addiction to them. We are quick to call anything we feel is unnatural a miracle. But what is unnatural in the first place? If something is occurring in nature, it must be natural! It may be infrequent, but it surely isn't unnatural or a miracle. There's a great presence sneaking around the edge of all of this just waiting for you to let it in. When you do, your life will significantly change for the better.

In closing his talk on the thinking mind, Ram Dass leaves us with these final words:

"Who you are isn't born nor dies, who you are neither comes nor goes. Who you are just is. You can't grasp it because you ARE it."

When you let go of the constraints your thinking mind creates and allow everything to unfold naturally, you are one step closer to The Everspace. However, even if we start to defeat the thinker and reduce the noise in our head, there will still be resistance to deal with. Resistance equates to fear and we need to know how to see through it.

161

The Resistor

When you start to understand the workings of your body and your mind in relation to the Universe, there's a certain power you start to feel that brings you freedom. You'll start to see that everything is perfect just as it is. You don't have to do anything, or be anybody, and everything just works itself out. Until one day it doesn't. This is when the resistor arrives. Something that we may consider to be bad, or unacceptable happens in our life and the first thought that comes through our mind is, "See, this shit doesn't work!" We instantly revert back to judging and resist our path. What we don't know is that the path to freedom requires complete surrender. Surrender to your body, surrender to your thoughts, and surrender to the outside world, or the actions of others.

In the book The War of Art (9) by Steven Pressfield he states, "Most of us have two lives. The life we live, and the unlived life within us. Between the two stands resistance." He then goes on to describe what he calls resistance's greatest hits. Let's look at a few, which I feel are relevant to this book:

1. The pursuit of any calling or creative art.
2. The launching of any new business.
3. The starting of any diet or health regimen.
4. Any program of spiritual advancement.
5. Education of every kind.
6. Any act that entails commitment of the heart.
7. The taking of any principled stand or facing adversity.

If you look closely at the concepts above, they all have one thing in common and that is they offer no immediate gratification, only long-term growth. No one thinks of, creates, and finishes a book or a painting in one day. Nor does one open a new business and become a millionaire the same day as well. All of these things take time and the road will be bumpy. The ego will tire quickly from things not going its way and soon it will make you want to quit. It will do anything and tell you anything to accomplish this. It will trick you, it will bully you, and if all else fails it will try to seduce you into getting what it wants. It will beg and plead and make itself seem so very real, but it is all an illusion. The way to finally get rid of it is not to fight it because that's what it wants. Fighting makes it stronger. What you have to do is just let it be. Like a screaming fussy child, when it does not get its way and nobody is listening to it, it will quiet itself.

Resistance, Pressfield says, "is fueled by our very own fear." It actually has no strength of its own; our fear gives it strength. When you are trying to control your ego, or defeat it, you may become fearful of who you will be without it. What will I be like? Who will protect me from getting hurt or being used? This is all new territory, which will produce fear. We will in a sense become more self-conscious and fearful moving forward because fear only allows you to measure what you will lose, not what you will gain. To combat this, we need to remember that we are part of nature and part of the Universe. All knowledge and direction is contained within us all you have to do is sit and listen. The first time I meditated, the fear was so great about losing some "part" of me I didn't want to lose I started crying. If you're strong enough to do that and you can sit and clear your mind, the fear starts to dissipate along with all of the anxiety, depression, irritations, job stresses, political fears, and unanswered questions. If you sit long enough and just breathe, all of these illusions are replaced with the answers you are looking for, the callings that you seek, and the next steps for improving your mind, body, and soul. Ram Dass says, "The Universe is conscious, not self-conscious. It does not know it knows, it just knows." We will never grow; never move forward in life if we fear taking a step towards what we do not know. This is where faith needs to enter our bloodstream and penetrate every cell. This is where mistakes can be learned. This is where our intuitive heart and mind become reinforced, and it is completely against how we are told to live today.

Usually, if we become sad, or angry, or depressed, we are either given a big pharma drug, or someone goes out and buys us something. You're not going to be happy once you get that new car, new dress, or dozen roses. Happiness comes before all of that and is what affords you the possibility of such things. To achieve goals in life we must be happy with the process like Nishkama Karma tells us. Tying your happiness to the end result of any goal will be cause for suffering. Like Buddha said, "We suffer when we get what we don't want, and we also suffer sometimes when we get what we do want." This is what happens when the thinker and the resistor get together. You say, "I want this!" But then you get it and you're like, "I didn't know it would be like this and I don't want it anymore." To help me stay centered, I read The Third Chinese Patriarch of Zen, which was written by Seng-ts'an around 590 A.D. every single day. While you can reflect on each line for quite some time, I like to read it in its entirety, and then I choose a verse which has a special meaning to me that day and reflect on it for 5 minutes or so. Here are just the first couple of lines, which illustrate so well what I am trying to help you understand:

"The Great Way is not difficult
for those who have no preferences.

When not attached to love or hate,
all is clear and undisguised.

Separate by the smallest amount, however,
and you are as far from it as heaven is from earth.

If you wish to know the truth,
then hold to no opinions for or against anything.

To set up what you like against what you dislike
is the disease of the mind.

When the fundamental nature of things is not recognized
the mind's essential peace is disturbed to no avail.

The Way is perfect as vast space is perfect,
where nothing is lacking and nothing is in excess.

Indeed, it is due to our grasping and rejecting
that we do not know the true nature of things.

Live neither in the entanglements of outer things,
nor in ideas or feelings of emptiness.

Be serene and at one with things,
and erroneous views will disappear by themselves.

When you try to stop activity to achieve quietude,
your very effort fills you with activity.

As long as you remain attached to one extreme or another
you will never know Oneness."

"The great way is not difficult to those who have no preferences." That line right there says everything. Having preferences invites resistance into your heart and mind. The author is not saying that you can't prefer a cheeseburger to a hamburger, what he's saying is to not be attached to the cheeseburger so you don't get upset if by accident you're served a hamburger, or worse yet a veggie burger. How many of us fly off the handle at the most trivial things? Our emotions run wild and we can't focus for the rest of the day because the person behind the counter served us the wrong type of coffee. It will be 5 p.m. and we will still be ready to tell anyone who will listen how a 20-something barista messed up your entire day. To the resistor, nothing is ever your fault. Your day, your month, and your life are the product of what others have done to you. There's no ownership in anything because responsibility means growth and growth means you are taking action and not resisting. You will resort to casting yourself as a victim, which is the antithesis of doing work! The resistor loves when you play the victim because then you will resort to talking about your problems constantly. If you are addicted to talking about your problems, if you complain about the same things every day, you must stop. Stop complaining even for just 24 hours, and watch how your life changes. Rather than trying to get other people to make you feel better, try making others feel better about themselves. Walk around and compliment people, even if it's just something trivial. Let them know you are at their service if they need anything. Most people will be so shocked they won't know what to do, but the sentiment is there. By helping someone else, you place value on their life, which is one of the greatest things you can do in this world.

I know by now I may have lost some of you. I'll watch my

ego you say, but telling someone else I am at his or her service, well that's just too far. It's not too far, it's necessary. Ask yourself this – do you want loneliness or freedom? If you desire loneliness, then practice being the victim. If you desire freedom, then help others. It's that simple. Nobody's beliefs will set them free, that is just the beginning and true change takes action. It's your behavior that sets you free.

The resistor will sit around and point out faults in everyone else too, ruining your relationship, and potential relationships. Once again everyone else is at fault and you are made to seem perfect. You can lose a lot of connections this way. Instead of working on being the ideal partner, or friend, we seek out who we think will be the perfect partner, which falls short eventually because our true self is seeking equality, not perfection, and if you don't love who you are, you'll never be able to love someone just like you. You'll find Mr. or Mrs. Perfect and then the resistor will spite their perfection, which will eventually drive them away. You cannot change other people. Whatever is providing resistance is the work that needs to be done in you. Husband won't help do the laundry? You need to learn how to selflessly LOVE doing laundry. Wife doesn't understand why you need to go out with the guys every Saturday night? You need to grow up, become an adult and realize being married means you have new priorities. The resistor projects the work onto other people. It will seek reinforcement from people you know will sympathize with you. It will trick you into thinking you are right because that's what you want to be.

There is no room for resistance in The Everspace. Sometimes you are handed tasks you have no idea how to complete. If you accept the task then the steps will unfold

167

along the way the deeper you go inward and make space for them to come out. If you decline the task, it will move onto someone else as Elizabeth Gilbert found out. If you resist the task however, the signal will stop and no more tasks will be given. When you convince yourself you can't do something, what you are saying is you haven't done it yet or you're too scared, or too worried to try. It's not you that's scared, it's your ego, and it's the resistor. It's the illusion you are creating to remain stuck in life looking for a savior, but no such savior exists. There are people that can help you, or point you in the right direction, but the actual process of waking up is going to come from inside of you, not outside.

All this mention of work must be making you sick by now. I have too much work you're thinking, and you may be right. The key to working on our ego however, is actually not working on it. The key to working on the ego is to cease doing work, and that means you guessed it, MEDITATION. If you think you don't have time to meditate I will have to quote one of my mentors, Mahatma Gandhi, when he said, "I have so much to accomplish today, that I must meditate for two hours instead of one." Just the very thought of "I don't have enough time" shows how sick and addicted our mind is to stuff, that we even RESIST the thought of just sitting. I even foreshadowed this when I told you in order to clear muddy water just leave it alone. It's the same for the ego. Within the first 20 minutes you will deal with all three ugly heads. Your back, butt, and knees may start to ache, and then thoughts will come pouring out causing you to drift, and lastly the resistor will show up and say "This is stupid, it's not working, let's go "do" something." The key to continuing will be to fall into love with yourself, and be gentle with everything you encounter. Love is a great

168

teacher with whom all of its lesson are free and can last a lifetime. Remember Swen Nater at the beginning of this lesson? He was so enamored by the love and care Coach Wooden showed for him, even though he didn't start a single game, that he sent Coach Wooden over 120 poems that he said were based off what he learned from him while playing basketball at UCLA. Here's just one you can ponder before starting the next lesson:

I Saw Love Once
I saw love once, I saw it clear.
It had no leash; it had no fear.
It gave itself without a thought.
No reservation had it bought.
It seemed so free to demonstrate.
It seemed obsessed to orchestrate,
A symphony, designed to feed,
Composed to lift the one in need.
Concern for others was its goal,
No matter what would be the toll.
It's strange just how much care it stores,
To recognize its neighbor's sores,
And doesn't rest until the day,
It's helped to take those sores away.
Its joy retains and does not run,
Until the blessing's job is done.
I saw love once; 'twas not pretend.
He was my coach; he is my friend.

We all want to be so influential in this world that people will write poems about us, but we have absolutely no idea how to access the abundance inside of us for The Everspace to flow through. Hopefully by now, the path is becoming clearer.

We are all suffering over something, but does this mean we have to make others suffer as well? Does this mean we have the right to broadcast our suffering for all of society to see? Does this mean we lock ourselves in our room and curl up into a little ball, thus playing the victim? All of these outlets are dead ends, or worse yet, serve to continue the drama. Suffering with grace means you are not attached to your suffering. It also means you're not wearing it like a big old bag of courage either. Sure, it's sad you lost a loved one or lived through a traumatic event, but you're not the only one, and I'm sure if you poked around the internet enough, you'll find some stories that make your feel like small potatoes. Having grace doesn't mean we refuse to feel, I'm a huge advocate of crying when you need to because of all of the physiological benefits it affords. It means suffering without LOOKING for sympathy. You can't play the victim and be in The Everspace, you need to practice acceptance.

There's no asking why this particular event had to happen because you already know; it was for your growth. Suffering with grace means holding your head up high and receiving condolences or help from loved ones or neighbors with a sense of gratitude and love. There was a priest who broke his leg once and everyone in the parish rushed to his home to see what they could do for him. After the first day the priest was overwhelmed and would no longer accept people into his home. His leg hurt, he was in a lot of pain and his pride had taken a hit. He was used to being the giver, not the receiver. It was a day or two after that when another parish member stopped by to bring him some food. He lost his temper and shunned the man away. The parish member looked at the priest and said, "Father, you have been helping all of us for years and we love you for it, being able to help you in your time of need allows us to show you that so we wish you would be more accepting of our gifts." The priest was humbled and immediately recognized he was wrong.

The moral of that story shows how in times of suffering we actually ENHANCE our separateness. We sometimes shut people out because we don't want to feel needy. So much of the American culture is about portraying strength and focuses on the triumph of the individual, but nobody in this world has truly made it alone. There's nothing wrong with accepting condolences, or other people's help. We just need to make sure our intentions are sincere and these gifts are not being exploited. Even Jesus grieved when he heard about the death of John the Baptist, yet after a short period of reflection he went back to curing the sick and feeding the poor.

Suffering with grace allows you to take up the duties you have before you, to give them up to the departed, to God, or to do them on behalf of the Universe. Wanting to be in The Everspace means refusing the right to self-pity, and at times suffering, we go alleviate the burdens of others.

Uncomfortability Challenge: Devote Yourself

Are you beginning to notice a pattern yet? All of these "Keys to The Everspace," and Uncomfortability Challenges are bringing us deeper and deeper into our hearts and further away from our minds. I'm not a hater of the mind, it's an amazing tool when you use it correctly, or just make sure you're using it, and it's not using you. These words

we are using – gratitude, faith, surrender, devotion – they all transcend the mind, don't they? There's a huge difference in saying, "He's devoted to her," compared to, "He's really loyal to her." I've had people in my life that were very loyal to me and the relationship still fell apart. I racked my brain over this for years trying to figure out where I went wrong and then suddenly it hit me.
I was devoted to them, but they weren't devoted to me.

Now I'm not saying that I'm better than they were in any sense and I'm definitely not trying to put them down. What we must realize is you can only meet someone as far as you have met yourself. Somewhere in my life I had realized and adopted this attitude of devotion. I would do anything for these people. I would give, and give, and give, and they would take everything I had to offer. Once they felt they didn't need my gifts anymore, they would drop me. This doesn't make them bad people, they just haven't met that part of themselves yet where devotion resides. Devotion comes from the heart, and loyalty comes from the mind. You say, "He's a very devoted follower" because you know he eats, sleeps and breathes whatever craft he is learning. It's Magic Johnson dribbling his basketball everywhere he went when he was young (10). It's Wayne Gretzky ice-skating for 8 to 10 hours a day when he was three years old (11). Devotion means having a heart-mind awareness to see anything through. Find something to devote yourself to. Find devoted friends and spouses. These are the people that will be with you through thick and thin. Align yourself with other people who share your values, don't impose your values on others. I've tried to explain these ideas to people before and some of them get it, and the rest just say they do but clearly can't connect deep enough for the idea to pass through them.

Devote yourself to your wife, your children, your job, your religion, or any other avenue that helps you work on yourself. If you can't think of anything, devote your life to service because like Zig Ziglar said, "You can have everything in life you want, if you will just help enough other people get what they want."

References:

1. Bill Walton. (n.d.). Retrieved November 22, 2016, from https://en.wikipedia.org/wiki/Bill_Walton
2. H. (2007). Swen Nater - Don Yaeger. Retrieved November 22, 2016, from http://donyaeger.com/swen-nater/
3. Vujicic, N. (n.d.). Bio - Life Without Limbs. Retrieved November 22, 2016, from https://www.lifewithoutlimbs.org/about-nick/bio/
4. Smith, R. (2016). 'Call me and talk to me like a man': Kanye West addresses former pal Jay Z in ANOTHER on-stage rant as he takes aim at rapper's wife Beyoncé, Hillary Clinton and Mark Zuckerberg... before ending show after 10 MINUTES. Retrieved November 22, 2016, from http://www.dailymail.co.uk/tvshowbiz/article-3953976/Kanye-West-rips-Beyonce-Hillary-Clinton-Mark-Zuckerberg-stage-rant-ending-concert-just-10-MINUTES-leaving-fans-fuming.html
5. Watts, A. (Producer). (2014, February 9). What Is [Audio podcast]. Retrieved from http://feeds.feedburner.com/zencast
6. Holiday, R. (2016). Ego is the enemy. NY, NY: Portfolio, Penguin.
7. Coelho, P. (2011). Aleph. UK, Harper Collins,
8. Dass, R. (Producer). (2016, March 7). The Thinking Mind [Audio podcast]. Retrieved from

http://ramdasshereandnow.libsyn.com/rss

9. Pressfield, S. (2012). The war of art: Break through the blocks and win your inner creative battles. New York: Black Irish Entertainment.

10. T. (n.d.). Earvin "Magic" Johnson - TheXtraordinary. Retrieved November 22, 2016, from http://www.thextraordinary.org/earvin-magic-johnson

11. (2014). Duhatschek: In the City of Angels, NHL mends fences with The Great One. Retrieved November 22, 2016, from http://www.theglobeandmail.com/sports/hockey/duhatschek-in-the-city-of-angels-nhl-mends-fences-with-the-great-one/article16320423/

EverLesson 6: Cultivating Conscious Love

"The Governments of the States Parties to this Constitution on behalf of their peoples declare: That since wars begin in the minds of men, it is in the minds of men that the defenses of peace must be constructed;

That ignorance of each other's ways and lives has been a common cause, throughout the history of mankind, of that suspicion and mistrust between the peoples of the world through which their differences have all too often broken into war;

That the great and terrible war which has now ended was a war made possible by the denial of the democratic principles of the dignity, equality and mutual respect of men, and by the propagation, in their place, through ignorance and prejudice, of the doctrine of the inequality of men and races;

That the wide diffusion of culture, and the education of humanity for justice and liberty and peace are indispensable to the dignity of man and constitute a sacred duty which all the nations must fulfill in a spirit of mutual assistance and concern;

That a peace based exclusively upon the political and economic arrangements of governments would not be a peace which could secure the unanimous, lasting and sincere support of the peoples of the world, and that the peace must therefore be founded, if it is not to fail, upon the intellectual and moral solidarity of mankind.

For these reasons, the States Parties to this Constitution, believing in full and equal opportunities for education for all, in the unrestricted pursuit of objective truth, and in the free exchange of ideas and knowledge, are agreed and determined to develop and to increase the means of communication between their peoples and to employ these means for the purposes of mutual understanding and a truer and more perfect knowledge of each other's lives."

-From The UNESCO Constitution

Innsbruck, Austria

Gitera The Farmer

In Howard Cutler's book with the Dalai Lama, The Art of
Happiness in a Troubled World (1), he tells us the story of
a man named Gitera who was a farmer in Rwanda, Africa.
It's early spring 1996 in the small town of Nyarubuye,
Rwanda where two different ethnic groups, Tutsis and
Hutus were residing side-by-side, living peacefully. Gitera,
a local farmer said, "Life was normal for the most part. As
long as we had a harvest large enough where we didn't
have to buy food from the market, people were happy." On
April 6th 1996, the Hutu president was murdered which
sparked a break in a cease-fire that was signed a year ago
between the two parties. The death of the president forced
all of the hatred and anger between the two parties to
surface, and it was not long before the systematic
genocide of the Tutsis began at the hand of the Hutus,
which were still in power at the time.

Nine days later Gitera found himself wielding a machete
covered with blood, chopping his next-door neighbors to
death inside the local church. Mothers, fathers, children,
he was hacking them all to pieces. The Tutsi people fled to
this church because they felt it was where they all learned
that murder was a sin. They sought refuge from what they
felt was still a common area between them. Instead over
seven thousand Hutu men surrounded the church and
slaughtered all who were inside. Gitera described a scene
of unimaginable horror saying, "People were running away
with their hands already amputated, there were people
rolling around in agony with no arms left, and no legs." He
said finally, "Those people were my neighbors."

This may seem like it was a spontaneous uprising, but in actuality it was planned for some time. Hutus were considered to be a little darker-skinned than Tutsis, and under the current government all Tutsis had to register and carry cards identifying them as so. Because of the high illiteracy rate, radio was a very influential way to get the message of genocide out. The majority Hutu population started using propaganda messages like stating all Tutsis are "cockroaches" and voices saying, "let's see what Tutsi women taste like."

The Rwandan Military along with Hutu militia paired up and forced all Hutu civilians to fight or "die like the Tutsis will." The Military handed out grenades and machetes to all Hutus that came to fight, but were reluctant to hand over any firearms, because in order to purchase firearms you needed a lot of paperwork, whereas grenades and machetes did not require any paperwork. This meant everything would be done up close and personal. Husbands were killing wives, wives were killing husbands, neighbors were killing neighbors, brothers and sisters were killing each other, and children were killing their parents. Out of a population of 7.3 million people—84% of whom were Hutu, 15% Tutsi and 1% Twa—the official figures published by the Rwandan government estimated the number of victims of the genocide to be 1,174,000 in 100 days (10,000 murdered every day, 400 every hour, 7 every minute (2)). For 100 days, hate fueled the minds of these human beings and as a result all social categories disappeared. There were no more friends, families, doctors, butchers, farmers, shoemakers, drug store owners, mechanics, or clergymen. There was only dead and alive, only us versus them. How does this happen? As horrible as this situation was, how can we pull anything good out of it? Here's the final shocking fact about this story: An estimated 20,000 children were conceived during sexual assaults while this genocide was taking place. Twenty thousand new lives were created while the senseless ending of over a million lives was taking place. Maybe one of those new lives will make a serious impact for the better on the world. Maybe one of those new lives will cure cancer or AIDS. It's all about perspective though. Looking at that positive fact, that somehow, life reproduced itself, or somehow balanced out its losses is a way to give meaning to what happened. It's a very small positive, and it's no way of reproducing the species, but the fact remains that life arose from rape, pillage, and murder.

The idea of hate is a very real threat no matter who you are, where you live, or what you are doing. What's most disturbing about hate crimes is that they never make any sense. Look at the story you just read about the genocidal killing in Rwanda. One minute you have a friend, the next minute you have pieces of a friend because you cut him up. You can say one thing for certain; hate has no enemies, it does not discriminate, and holds no prejudices. I've experienced hate, as I'm sure you have too, but what people don't understand is hate is not an expression, it's actually a closing of the heart and mind to what is. It's the Resistor in its worst form.

In Mitch Albom's book The Five People You Meet In Heaven (3) he puts into perspective what hate does when it manifests. He states, "All parents damage their children and create a sense of resentment. What the children fail to realize is that hate is a double-edged sword; the pain you think you are inflicting on someone else, you are actually inflicting on yourself (3)." Thoughts of hate arise from our ego structure and its ability to separate yourself from others. When you truly believe and accept this non-dualistic approach to nature, hate will simply start to fade away on its own. Ram Dass says, "Treat everyone like God in drag," meaning see God in everyone you meet, not just the cute cuddly kids, or the hot security cop at the mall. In order for hate to disappear you need to see God in the asshole that just cut you off, or the bitch that just spilled her drink on you, because that's where your next lesson took place. You think you own the road? Guess again, says God. You think that shirt makes you look special, or it's really important? Here, take a Cosmo to your precious shirt, says God! Hate is a sign we are taking something way too seriously and need to slow down, center ourselves, and come back to oneness with what is.

The best illustration of the foolishness of hate is when we hate objects, or worse yet, normal situations of life. How many people sit in their car on the highway, which turns into a parking lot during rush hour, and say to themselves, "I hate traffic!" What does that even mean? Do you expect no other cars to be on the road? Now we see the futility of the ego. We see how childish it really is. At the same time this person is sitting in traffic, they are trying to load Facebook, or Instagram (along with a thousand other people) using cellular data, and it's slow. The anxiety boils over because the ego does not want to live in the present moment so you now proclaim, "I hate how slow my phone is!" Do you think the phone or cell phone companies care?

All this closing off of present circumstances that we can learn from and merge with are lessons in acceptance. Acceptance is what allows us to keep our hearts open so feelings and emotions caused by life situations can pass through us and don't get stuck, blocking our accessibility of The Everspace. If we practice this long enough, what arises out of us is what I call Conscious love. Conscious love is not unconditional love. Like I said earlier, in today's day and age it is important to set boundaries for love in relationships because we all have conditions under which we will not love, but we don't communicate that to our partner. Unconditional love is something that is largely reserved for those who obtain enlightenment, and I'll be the first to admit I'm just not there yet. I would consider conscious love to be one step below and needs to be the state at which we operate on a daily basis. In order to love others, we first need to love ourselves, and shockingly, not too many of us are brought up sharpening the sword of that skill.

The Art of Loving You

There isn't anybody in the world that Robin McLaurin Williams couldn't make laugh. With his boxy stature, long hairy arms, and somewhat scrunchy face, the man was obviously born to be a comedian. From Mork and Mindy to The Fisher King, Awakenings, What Dreams May Come and then Dead Poets Society, and Good Will Hunting, it seemed his talents had no boundaries. Robin Williams seemed like he was the type of guy you could drop off at a party of either 6-year-olds or 60-year-olds and he would make them all laugh, cry, and take their breath away multiple times before the night was over.

With a career spanning over 30 years, Williams had much to be proud of. He had been in over 50 movies, he's done countless stand-up comedy routines, won 30 + awards, and was nominated for said awards over 50 times. He had a net worth of around 130 million dollars, but spiritually, he was broke. Williams battled depression, drugs, and alcoholism most of his life. He was the epitome of addiction, but not the type of addiction you're thinking of in relation to substances. He was addicted to seeking a connection to something outside of himself. One of his quotes plastered all over the Internet shortly after he committed suicide is his tell-all:

"I used to think the worst thing in life was to end up all alone. It's not. The worst thing in life is to end up with people who make you feel all alone."

It seems as though Robin Williams could connect with any person on this planet, but yet he couldn't connect to himself. I have never been diagnosed as being clinically depressed, but I think I can state that when one is depressed their opinion of themselves is not a very high one. While Williams had a tremendous ability to love others, it seems he fell short on his ability to love himself. Kyle Cease is a comedian turned transformation artist. This is my name not his. Kyle's gig is called Evolving Out Loud and is primarily centered on workshop weekends where he speaks off the cuff about evolving your consciousness. No script, no plans, he just says whatever comes to his mind next and is a tremendous example of what someone looks like when they do work through The Everspace. During his YouTube video called The Big Talk he says, "Your circumstances in your life are a mirror of what you feel inside (4)." While most of us that are not working on our egos on a daily basis might not agree, Kyle is completely correct. Love attracts love and in return attracts positivity. It doesn't prevent bad things from happening; it allows you to transcend them when they do. The ability for us to love anything in this world starts with the ability to love ourselves. It means if we make a mistake we don't then become mad, or hate ourselves, creating years of regret. Self-love is always treating yourself first and foremost with gentleness, and respect. I was with a girlfriend one who had forgotten her wallet at home and we were on our way to a movie. She lived 30 minutes in the opposite direction we were going so there was no going back to get it. "I can't believe how stupid I am," she proclaimed and with that I had to teach her a lesson about tenderness to oneself. I asked her how she would feel if I called her stupid, or if someone else did, and she didn't like that idea very much. What makes it different that you called yourself stupid? I asked. She couldn't answer that question either.

Self-love begins with the voice in our head and the opinion of our self. It's not saying you're better than anybody else, it's saying, "I'm going to be the best version of myself that I can be today and every day." There's no competition to be had here. You're not trying to outdo others. From morning to noon to night, it's treating others with love and respect because you love and respect yourself. We are all reflections of one another, and you will receive whatever you project. People who are constantly under tension unknowingly push people away. When you are in a state of self-love, you constantly feel light. The entire world could collapse and you would just sit back and marvel at it all knowing that you will be all right. Fear is easily created by a lack of self-love because we project this lack in relationships and situations which in turn causes us to look for fulfillment elsewhere when it is inside us! We look for reinforcement in the form of approval from co-workers, parents, siblings, friends, people on Instagram, Twitter and Facebook, and when we don't receive what we are looking for, it sends our world into a tailspin. In August of 2015 I sat next to a girl on a flight from Toronto to Ft. Lauderdale. Before the flight took off she pulled her tray table out, placed an opened book on it, took a picture of it and posted it to Instagram. She then proceeded to put the book back in her bag, put the tray table up and then slept for the entire flight. I was quite saddened by this. I thought about how this girl must live in a constant state of anxiety, trying to come up with scenarios to post that will keep her followers accepting her. She's thinking that if she doesn't love who she is, then others won't as well, and in turn she needs to create a life of envy. Living in this constant state of envy production takes us further and further from our true self. Pretty soon our entire life becomes a lie. We portray ourselves as how we want to be seen, rather than how we truly are, and because we are not living from the heart which is where true creation comes from, the lies become limited because it is limited only to the mind's ability.

The thinking mind sees the heart as a threat because the heart knows that if you love yourself first, steps will unfold naturally for you to expand that love. The mind is saying, NOT SO FAST! I don't operate like that. I need to know what we are doing every step of the way. I need certainty that this all going to work out! It needs to approve of what you are doing. The mind is acting from its idea of somebody-ness, and if you think you're somebody, that means you can get hurt, or be taken advantage of. To the heart, you are nothing but a giver of infinite love. You are nobody, and being nobody means nothing can be taken from you. We are taught that to be somebody you need to use your mind in order to lead and become recognized, yet when you love yourself, or lead a heart-centered life, you become led by this infinite space where all possibility resides. You're going based on feeling, and that feeling is your precursor to faith. Jiddu Krishnamurti, an Indian philosopher and author once said, "Freedom is precisely the state of not having to choose." Isn't that where we all want to be? Instead of sitting around in fear wondering what we should do, wouldn't we all like to wake up every day and KNOW what we should do? Freedom from choice can only occur when we give up control, and giving up control is very hard for the egoist-thinking mind because it wants to care what others think about you. It wants to be able to control the amount of love you can extract from someone. It doesn't know that you ARE love. The heart only knows that, and when you start loving yourself, the love you deserve will manifest in form and find YOU, you won't have to find IT. It is at that point when you become truly free. You no longer become a seeker of things; you become a finder of things. Fortune just shows up at your doorstep and drops things off. Thoughts, words, and ways of thinking are rearranged for you to find the good in everything. I know once again how utopian this sounds. It's crazy, its cosmic, it's unsatisfactory says the brain, but the heart is just sitting there shaking its head in agreement.

In 2012 a neurosurgeon by the name of Eban Alexander wrote a book called *Proof of Heaven*. In it, he tells the story of how his brain and spinal cord became infected with E. coli, which put him into a coma, and he was pronounced clinically dead. During this time, he believes he visited what we humans consider to be heaven. He talks about the space he was in and says, "You are loved and cherished. You have nothing to fear. There is nothing you can do wrong. If I had to boil this entire message down to one sentence, it would run this way: You are loved. And if I had to boil it down further, to just one word, it would (of course) be, simply: Love (5)." We can obtain this same space here on Earth, but nobody is going to come and hand it to you because it is already inside of you. To obtain The Everspace, all you have to do is open your heart to what is.

Love Your Body

By the age of 13 I started to have terrible knee pain. My mother took me to a bunch of different doctors and none of them could find anything wrong. For the next 17 years, I exercised rigorously nearly every single day with the most incredible pain radiating from my knees. Sitting in cars for long periods of time was torture. I hated my knees. I cursed them every day. Is it any wonder that both of them blew out on me and needed to be surgically repaired? There is increasing evidence showing how negative emotions can actually cause disease, or other physiological problems in the body. In the book, Freedom From Pain: Discover Your Body's Power To Overcome Physical Pain, the authors state:

"We know that thoughts literally change brain chemistry. Research indicates that the chemical composition of the body can change in relation to a specific thought within 20 seconds (6)."

They then go on to say:

"If we are really focused on a thought or limiting belief, our nervous system will send messages almost immediately to our muscles which will then constrict (6)."

Now, just because you have short eyelashes and you hate them, does that mean that if you love them they will start growing? Who knows? All we do know is that by having negative thoughts about them, your body will send negative signals. Both of my knees are deformed now but guess what, I've learned to love them and they no longer cause me any pain. I can do anything I want now with my legs pain-free. The key was opening up and relaxing my quadriceps, which were so tight from all of the negative comments I used to give myself. Love your imperfections; they are what make you unique. Stop comparing yourself to the people in magazines or on TV, they have a village of people to make sure they look flawless. This is not optimal for anyone living outside of Hollywood. Eat well, exercise, and love your body through the entire process.

Love Your Thoughts

Love your thoughts. All of them. Especially the crazy ones. At times when I'm meditating or even if I'm walking or sitting around, a random thought will pop into my head that I would deem totally insane. Before, these thoughts would grab me, or more to the point, I would grab it and this would create fear. Now when these thoughts occur I look at it like a comedy show. Everybody loves comedy shows, right? I'll think something crazy and then right after that thought I say to myself, "That was cool! I wonder where the heck that came from?" Observation and love kill negative thoughts. They just pass through you on their way to another person's brain cell hoping they will grab it. You can't fake this love though. It needs to be genuine or else your fake form of love will turn to resistance and that thought just won't leave. You need to realize that the thought is not you that you are the space that thought came from. Loving that space allows the thought to be what it is. No judgment, no clinging, and then it will pass. Another way to do this is to actually do an experiment of the thought. I got this from author Tim Ferriss. When I knew I was going to shut my gym down, all these thoughts ran through my mind. What if I lose my home? What if I lose my car? Where am I going to get money? Underneath all of that my brain was equating no job with being homeless, so I experimented with being homeless one weekend. I slept in my gym on a massage table (which oddly becomes very uncomfortable after one hour) and allowed myself only $10 for food the whole weekend. No phone, no cable TV. I went to the beach and spent time at the library reading odd books. For food I survived on one coffee and a double whopper with fries each day. Was I uncomfortable? Sure. But I quickly realized that there wasn't anything to be afraid of in those living conditions. When I went back to my apartment on Sunday night and went to sleep, I woke up on Monday without a care in the world.

Love Your Resistance

Resistance brings pain. You know you have to rake the leaves up after school before you can go play video games with your friends. You get home, look at the chaos that is your yard and think, "I'll do it after playing video games, before Mom and Dad get home." Then Mom either gets home early, or you're having so much fun that you forget, and as you're walking home you see the yard and your heart sinks knowing you're going to get a whoopin'. I have found that I resist a lot of silly things because I feel they are going to be hard, or because I feel the task is beneath me, and every time I end up doing said task, I realize it wasn't as bad as I thought. In Brian

Tracy's book Eat That Frog! he says, "The hardest part of any important task is getting started on it in the first place. Once you actually begin work on a valuable task, you seem to be naturally motivated to continue (7)." I agree with this whole-heartedly and it applies in nearly every situation. Whether it's filing your taxes, quitting a job or starting a new one, or breaking up with a boyfriend, if you're resisting it, loving it will get you started. It breaks the chains and gets you progressing forward again. Most people say just grit your teeth and do it! But this implies the experience is going to be negative and nobody wants to have a negative experience. From the very beginning your heart and mind are bracing for the worst. Allow the resistance to melt into love where all things are possible. In order to progress closer to The Everspace we need to FALL IN LOVE with uncertainty.

When you feel uncertain about something, it is more than likely that you have never done it before. Embracing that uncertainty and having the courage to love not knowing where you are going or where you are going to end up not only makes the possibilities of your life endless, but also adds spontaneity and valuable life experience to your being. People have 5-year plans, 10-year plans, and then there are many people who need to have a plan in order to step foot out of the house. I'm not saying you should never plan, or that plans are bad, I'm saying when uncertainty arises with your plan, rather than resisting or throwing in the towel become curious about why life is leading you down this path. Even if you make the most horrendous of mistakes, that life experience was something you needed to know at that time. How many of us sit around scared to death of making a mistake and then find out at 60 years old we don't really know anything? Mistakes are God's way of teaching you how to evolve. They're life's way of not allowing you to get stuck. I'm a gym rat turned author. I have no idea whether this is going to be a sustainable way for me to live, but if someone asks me 10 years from now if I ever thought about writing a book, I can dust one off and hand it to them. So many of us get frustrated, or irritated with our resistance to things they carry over into our personal lives. We come home and yell at our wife or kick the dog because we're uncertain about this or about that. One of the best quotes I ever heard about this was from a mentor of mine Raul Villacis. He said, "Not making a decision is a decision." The wealthiest people in the world are where they are because they have made decisions, made mistakes, and learned from them. We must remember that our beings are infinite. Birth is the opposite of death, life goes on forever. All things are contained within us, the first step is believing in that fact. The problem is that we grow up being told what we are good at so we confine ourselves to labels. Along comes this voice saying, "Hey, you should make clay pots" but you dismiss it and resist the voice because Aunt Bonnie said you clearly have a knack for electronics, and as you stock the shelves day after day at BestBuy, you soon start to resist that and resent Aunt Bonnie because this feeling in your heart won't go away that you are not living your life's true purpose.

Love Your Vulnerability

There's a common underlying theme in life that we all partake in every day and it's called union. All we want to do is belong. We wear certain clothes, buy specific cars, and even shape our hair hoping that we will be liked and accepted by others. It's doesn't matter if one person likes you or twenty-five, we breed ourselves to be accepted. With acceptance comes vulnerability. We now worry about whether the clothes we are wearing are trendy, the car we drive is current, or if the part looks better on the left side of our head or the right. Like I said, all of this comes from a deep need for acceptance, but once again we are missing the mark because acceptance will come from without, if it is present within. Did you ever hear someone say, "She's such a strong woman!"? What's being referenced is her character, the way she holds herself in all situations. If you love where you are vulnerable you become impenetrable from the outside, and then nothing can hurt you. No amount of dirty stares, or negative comments will sway your mood.

In Brené Brown's TED Talk on vulnerability, she goes through fascinating data she collected for over 6 years while trying to research vulnerability. She says the less you want to talk about it, the more you have it. I found that fascinating because there are times where I will say something about death and you will have at least one person be particularly mortified. I just think, "Aren't we all vulnerable to death?" But this person doesn't even want to think about it. That person needs to exert high levels of love towards their vulnerability of death. Tibetan monks actually spend time meditating about their own deaths to reduce their fear of it. Brown went on to discover through over 1000 pieces of data that there were two groups at play. One that had a sense of love and belonging and another group that didn't. The only difference was that the group that had a sense of love and belonging BELIEVED they were worthy of it (8). They believed that what made them vulnerable made them beautiful. They believed in the need to say, "I love you" first. They believed in doing something that provided no guarantees. They believed in treating themselves with compassion because if you don't know how to treat yourself with compassion, then you won't know how to treat others with compassion, which loses your connection to them. Brown says vulnerability is a strength because it is the birthplace of joy, creativity, belonging and love. In America however, Brown says we numb vulnerability. She points out that today we are the most in debt, overweight, addicted, and medicated generation in American history, and as we try to numb our vulnerability we also numb emotions such as gratitude, and happiness which erodes our sense of meaning and belonging in the world. This parallels with our earlier idea of Wetiko. The more objects we buy, and the more brain cells we kill, the less confidence we have that our life has value, and that sends the heart into complete panic mode.

Conscious love

When I was younger, I was never a people person. Then one day, I realized I was a walking contradiction. Not only did my work consist of helping people, it was solely dependent on them for me to thrive. I realized that at the time that I did not like people very much. I also didn't like myself. I was constantly looking in the mirror wishing my hair looked more like Brad Pitt's, and I didn't like having such long legs. I noticed these things in other people as well. I either made fun of them, or just avoided them all together. Whatever the case, the judgments were there. When you really start to master the art of loving yourself you will notice a very profound shift happen in your life. You will start to effortlessly love others. This is what I call conscious love. Before we go into further detail, I know I said it once, but let me say it again. This is not unconditional love and you will see why in a moment. If you have the ability to love unconditionally then that's amazing, but I suspect those who have it do not need to read this book anyway. I'm sure they are fully immersed in The Everspace. Conscious love means that you are consciously projecting love to all that you meet. You no longer find flaws in other people; in fact, you see their flaws as beautiful. Rather than feeling sorry for those who are homeless or down on their luck, you feel empathy because you realize that may be the path they chose to become free. Instead of joining in on the company drama, or listening to gossip, you just smile and walk away without giving it a second thought. When you love consciously, you're not doing, you're just being with what is. Everything is OK. You could be in the middle of a Black Friday frenzy, or sitting on a secluded park bench. You watch life as it unfolds and you love it all, good or bad. You love the people kicking and screaming and you love the quirky people who get in your way. When your heart remains this wide open, you become open to everything. Nothing gets shut out, nothing gets stuck; it all is allowed to pass through you. Because of this you will start to attract many things your way and sometimes this may lead you into a trap.

The Love Trap

Believe it or not, there are actually people in the world today who will use other people's love against them. This makes it challenging when you're walking around as a gigantic ball of love and acceptance and ultimately will lead you into what I call the love trap. Family members will do this, friends will do this, and spouses will do this. Sometimes they are doing it consciously, and sometimes they are doing it unconsciously. Love trappers have not yet been taught how to love themselves, so they look for what they think they are lacking in others, and they use love as a means for keeping that person around. They will use terms like, "You know I love you, right?" Then they will turn around and act in way that are not becoming of love. A good example is domestic abuse. If you love someone, there should be nothing that person can do that would make you so mad that they deserve a beating. Women often claim they know their partner loves them as they are spitting blood out of their mouth talking to the cops. They will convince themselves to stay for the kids, or because they have a nice house. If you are being physically, mentally, or emotionally abused you are not living in The Everspace. Change is never difficult; it is dealing with change that is difficult. No amount of material possessions is worth someone making you feel unworthy of love. It's just that simple. If you are being used or abused, you need to express to this person how you feel. You need to have respect for yourself, and have empathy for the offender. Advise them how you feel and help them realize that things need to change or you can no longer be in the relationship. Sticking around and using love as an excuse breeds what psychologists call codependency.

Codependency is where you have "others' esteem" rather than self-esteem, where your emotions basically run on the feelings of others. Often times you trick yourself into thinking you are portraying unconditional love and end up craving that same love from your partner, but what relationship lasts when two people are hurting each other or taking advantage of each other's love? Your relationship becomes a ticking time bomb.
There's a thin line between non-duality and the love trap. Self-love has a certain robustness to it which gives you the ability to say no to someone while still keep your heart

open to them. Most people equate no with rejection or negativity, but when you say no to something or someone, what you are doing is refusing to be anything other than what you are. This authenticity will actually strengthen your relationship, not hinder it because you are not pretending to be someone or something you are not. People also question whether saying no enhances our feelings of separateness, but this is also false. The answer lies in spiritual maturity. There are many different levels of spirituality in today's world. Some people work on their spirit every day, while others only once a week, and some not at all. Through practice we all develop different levels of spiritual maturity. Some people can be 50 years old and still have the spirit of a child. They'll try to control others, hoard all of their money and possessions, and be love trappers, all while using the cover of a church-going Catholic. They will try to manipulate you as a child does to get what they want. There should be no judgment from you, just recognize it for what it is and don't play along in their games. Respond kindly with "no, thank you" or the like. It is not your job to "fix" this person; they just haven't done enough work yet to connect with themselves as deep as you are connecting with yourself. Other people can be very young, but play the game of life straight up. They don't lie, cheat, or steal, and will be the first ones to own up to their mistakes. They may or may not be church going, yet they know how to treat others fairly, and they live a heart-centered life. Just as we have physical and emotional maturity, when we are looking for a life mate, spiritual maturity needs to be taken into account as well.

Ram Dass said, "I work with others as a way of working on myself. We were all born from unconditional love; we are here on Earth to experience the conditions of it." Human emotions are difficult to work with, but by understanding the level of love you have for yourself, you set boundaries on your willingness to help others achieve their spiritual awakening or realization of The Everspace.

Bliss VS Happiness

When you grasp this idea of conscious love and it actually becomes a part of you, what you will then start to experience is unlimited happiness, or what people in the East call Bliss. Bliss is very challenging to put into words because it is a state of being, rather than a feeling. Happiness is a component of bliss, but it is not its foundation, because worldly events still have the potential to disrupt you. You can be happy that you're going to see your friend after 7 years, but then that happiness can become eroded when your flight gets cancelled or things don't go as planned. Bliss is living your life as though nothing is to your advantage or disadvantage. Life is being life and you're just happy to be alive. It is the true art of complete acceptance to what is, and undying love for uncertainty. It's being as curious about what the next moment will bring for the growth of your spirit as a little boy unwrapping presents on Christmas morning. Nothing can disappoint you because there are no expectations, only the flow of life, and because you are flowing with life, all things become afforded to you. Think about it in this way. Unhappiness is like swimming against the current of a river; it's a lot of work for little reward. Happiness is just floating in the river; you don't have to do too much work to get where you want to go. But bliss is like swimming with the current of the river, which allows you to use your power AND the power of the river!

People who experience bliss don't run around talking about it, updating their status with it, or tweeting about it because bliss arises from conscious love and the product of love is listening, not talking. Talking is what the ego does; it wants to show everyone how much it knows so it can be admired. Love records, it doesn't recite. Love admires! Love doesn't say look at me, it says look at you! When you are in this state is when you are blissful, because you know that no matter what someone else accomplishes, nothing is reduced from you. Some people fear the accomplishments of others. They can be happy, but that happiness is dependent upon the mind's satisfaction. When that person starts to compare or think someone else has more than they do, fear kicks in and happiness erodes.

Bliss comes from deep within us that worldly events cannot touch. We can still experience pain and sadness. Bliss doesn't mean we are untouchable; it's like the sun behind the clouds just waiting to beam light down upon us when we choose to see it. Contrast this with someone who doesn't believe in bliss where they walk around in a continuous state of hopelessness and despair. Bliss is your reward for learning life's lesson. If it's loss, we learn the impermanence of life and to not take it for granted, if it's pain we learn the frailty of life, if it's fear we learn to love uncertainty. When you learn, you are immediately brought back to a state of restfulness and peace. Bliss allows you to not live according to preconceived notions of what spirituality really means. It's not living without expressing any feelings; it's learning to express them to the fullest knowing you'll return to love when they run their course. Bliss is an eraser of fear; it allows you to feel what you need when you need it knowing you won't get stuck there. Accepting bliss in your life makes you the bulletproof, rock-solid, unfuckwithable human being you were born to be.

Your Key To Accessing The Everspace: Forgiveness

Renowned author Neale Donald Walsch once said, "The Universe sent you nothing but angels." Forgiveness is one of the most powerful tools we have. In America, only the religious are preaching forgiveness. Everyone else, especially if you're in the business world, is preaching revenge. Forgiveness is a tool we use to break the chains of mental slavery and unlock our past, allowing it to drift on down the river. Hanging on to how you have been hurt, or who wronged you, stops your ability to live in the present. Just when you think you have suppressed all of these feelings of hurt, you hear this person's name again, see them on Instagram, or get a text from them and you just cringe. All of those old feelings resurface like it happened yesterday. When we forgive, it doesn't necessarily mean we have to forget, all it means is we broke the emotional ties, or got off the emotional roller coaster. Forgiveness is giving up the feeling that you have been hurt.
Whether the action was done on purpose or by accident is irrelevant. The best way to deal with this is compassion. Maybe they hurt you because someone else hurt them. Use compassion to rid yourself of these feelings because they are weighing you down and the negativity is blocking your happiness and access to The Everspace. You can never control other people's reactions, only your own. This is not being weak, as it would be easier to just tell someone to screw off and be done with them. Practicing compassion is a heart-centered emotion. As you gain greater conscious abilities, YOU have the duty to act from a higher power. This power is your heart, not your mind,

so the more people that hurt you, the more you use your heart, and the more your spirit grows. Forgiveness, therefore, is not your gift to them; it is their gift to you.

Uncomfortability Challenge

Call up someone whom you feel has wronged you and ask him or her to get a coffee with you one morning. If they decline, no worries, move on to the next person. Start off with smaller offenders if you want, then work your way up to the biggies. Make sure you have done all of the work in your heart to forgive them first, and when you go to meet them, pretend you are meeting them for the first time. Make the meeting as long or as short as you wish. Ask him or her questions about work, their favorite color, or what life was like in College. Notice their humanness, notice how everyone, every day is walking around scared shitless, hoping that what they are doing is right. Who knows, maybe the first person you take to go get coffee is yourself so you can release all of the guilt that has been eating you away inside for something you were never taught how to deal with. Sometimes the first person we need to forgive is ourselves.

References:

1. B., & Cutler, H. C. (2009). The art of happiness in a troubled world. New York: Doubleday.
2. (n.d.). Retrieved November 29, 2016, from https://en.wikipedia.org/wiki/Rwandan_genocide
3. Albom, M. (2003). The five people you meet in heaven. New York: Hyperion.
4. Kyle Cease - The Big Talk
5. Alexander, E. (2012). Proof of heaven: A neurosurgeon's journey into the afterlife. New York: Simon & Schuster.
6. Levine, P. A., & Phillips, M. (2012). Freedom from pain: Discover your body's power to overcome physical pain. Boulder, CO: Sounds True.
7. Tracy, B. (2007). Eat that frog!: 21 great ways to stop procrastinating and get more done in less time. San Francisco, CA: Berrett-Koehler.
8. Brene' Brown - The Power of Vulnerability

EverLesson 7. Finding Your True Self

"Everything has been figured out. Except how to live."

-Jean-Paul Sartre

"Do not believe in anything because it is said. … nor in the mere authority of your teachers or masters…. Believe when the writing, doctrine, or saying is corroborated by your reason and consciousness."

-Buddha

201

The Universe Inside

Alan Watts gave an amazing talk called, "The Space (Universe) You Don't See Inside You." Not only is the talk absolutely amazing, but the title is very fitting as well. In the talk, he says, "If God were visible, nobody would be able to see anything but God, but by the virtue of God being invisible, the world is created. God gets out of the way and the world becomes a selection. The eyes select what they want to see, and the consciousness becomes selective as well." For the most part, our consciousness is developed through our childhood. What we learn becomes known to us, what we touch becomes real, and what we think becomes absolute. The problem is that there are certain instances that occur in our life where "thinking" does not solve what we are looking for. It seems at times the reality of this world is here to trick us, or keep us guessing. Lao Tzu said, "Without going outside my house, I can know the whole Universe." What Lao Tzu is saying is that for us to really "know" something, we must turn inside to learn, not outside.

Even the most profound thinkers of antiquity agree we are all connected through some type of fabric. This fabric can't be measured by science, but it is believed to exist. Most people believe that if our five senses (sight, touch, hearing, smell, taste) cannot contact something, then it isn't real. The problem with this is that it leaves nothing unexplained; yet there is much occurring in this world that cannot be explained. Take for instance the Aspect Experiment in France that demonstrated how two once-connected quantum particles separated by light year

202

distances remained somehow connected. If one particle was changed, the other changed instantly. Scientists don't know the mechanics of this, but it is dubbed spooky action at a distance, which is information that travels faster than the speed of light in violation of special relativity, and shows that non-locality and non-causality can be aspects of physical reality. Some theorists suggest that this connection requires a higher understanding of life and its dimensions than we know of right now. This problem was discovered in 1982 and we still don't have an answer yet! They are getting closer though. An experiment called OPERA (Oscillation Project with Emulsion-tRacking Apparatus) was just conducted in Italy with atomic structures called Neutrinos. Neutrinos are neutrally charged particles that have little to no mass. They are bouncing around everywhere, every day and you have no idea they are there. The sun produces so many Neutrinos as a by-product of nuclear reactions that many billions can pass through your eye every second and you can't even tell. The scientists in Italy took a concentration of Neutrinos and shot them to a metal plate in Geneva, Switzerland. To the researchers' amazement, the Neutrinos arrived an average of 60 nanoseconds faster than the light particles in over 16,000 experiments! String theorists are saying the Neutrinos are slipping through extra dimensions in space not identified yet. Einstein's theory of relativity, by which all scientists base their findings, may be incomplete. After hearing all this information, is it so hard to believe that we are connected, rather than separate, from all of life, and that the full spectrum of consciousness may encompass both physical and non-physical dimensions of reality?

We have said much about intuition in this book and I bet some of you are just not quite sold on the idea yet. The fact of the matter is that as human beings we are becoming exponentially smarter about how the Universe works, but in the process becoming less and less in tune with nature, its vibrations, and its energy. We allow apps and computers to think and do things for us, and since the mind has no responsibility, it preoccupies itself with any type of entertaining smut it can find. Videos of cute cats and dancing babies occupy most of our days and distract us from what our spirit desires, which is to grow in awareness. On December 26th, 2004, a Tsunami struck the southern coast of India eliminating 230,000-310,000 human lives, yet only a few dead Buffalo were found and one dead cat. There are many accounts from survivors about how animals were seen fleeing inland or behaving strangely on the morning of the 26th. One person reported his dogs would not go running with him on the beach that morning, and zookeepers noticed the monkeys going on the fritz and not eating their bananas. FOX news called it a 6th sense, but Diana Reiss, Ph.D., director of marine mammal research at the Wildlife Conservation Society said "I don't think it's a sixth sense — at least nothing we can measure at this point." Nothing we can measure? Once again this is a denial of any type of dimension other than the physical.

The animals "knew" the Tsunami was coming. How did they know? Were they watching an animal news broadcast we don't have access to? It's the same with hurricanes. When hurricanes hit tropical areas, all of the birds disappear. Once again, I don't think any of them have the capability to watch CNN. Scientists theorize that birds can hear infrasounds, which are frequencies below 20Hz, and these sounds may be made by wind, barometric pressure, or waves crashing out in the distance. Like I said though this is just a theory.

Scientists don't completely know how the birds know, but the birds definitely know. What you are about to find out is that there's a lot you know as well; you just don't know that you know because you're too busy knowing something else, and this is the clutter that gets in the way of The Everspace, and you living the life you want to.

21st-Century Addictions

We are human and do things for enjoyment. Addictions are sneaky little buggers that distract us from living in the present moment, and allowing us to reach a deeper connection with life. In the roaring 20's it was alcohol, then in the 60's and 70's it was drugs. Much has been said about these two paths to addiction, and is beyond the scope of this book, so they will not be covered here. Instead, we are going to discuss addiction to sugar, porn, and our phones, all of which have a very cloudy grey area that not too many people are talking about. Addiction to alcohol or drugs is pretty clear; usually the person ends up being a mess and can no longer control their life. But how do you know when you're addicted to sugar? Or porn? Or your cell phone? It is these three factors I believe are distracting us from connecting to ourselves in today's society, making us less aware of nature, in exchange for popularity in a virtual world. We eat fake food with no real nutrition, we admire false ideas of what someone else thinks sex is, and we trade genuine conversation for likes, status updates, and 10-second chats.

If you think addiction, or even heavy reliance upon these things is not a big deal, you need to think again because they are all blocking you from hearing, or feeling what The Everspace is trying to send through you. We must keep in mind that addiction doesn't necessarily mean how much you're performing an action; it's also how much you're thinking about it too. This obsessive thinking turns to the reward center of our brain to be satisfied, which makes us a bunch of people walking around with happy brains, but crummy, unfulfilled lives.

W-M-D

Dopamine is the limbic system's weapon of mass destruction. Any time we act on a pleasurable thought, dopamine is released into the prefrontal cortex, which is responsible for self-control and willpower, personality, and decision-making (i.e. awareness). Dopamine may stimulate the reward center of our brain, but I assure you no reward is provided. Instead of a reward, dopamine provides a stimulus for arousal which means the next time you see, hear, smell, touch or taste something there's a direct link in the brain that says, "I like that, get some!" Dopamine is an antenna for desire. It makes you seek, crave and want something that is not necessarily readily available. It's a distractor from the present moment, and a huge key to addictive behaviors. Scientists used to think people were born predisposed to addiction, which can be true if previous generations of family members were addicted too, but how do you explain being addicted to something, when there are no previous addictions present in your family tree? For the last fifteen years, scientists have been hot on the trail of a transcription factor called Delta FosB. Transcription factors are proteins that convert DNA to RNA in our body. What they are finding out is that every time dopamine is released due to some type of drug (for the record, I am classifying sugar, porn, and cell phones as drugs here), Delta FosB gets triggered, which then makes us more sensitive to that stimulus wanting more. At the same time our brain starts to become numbed in a sense to the same levels of dopamine, which creates constant arousal, beginning the cycle of addiction. In an experiment done by Eric J. Nestler at The University of Texas, he showed that Delta FosB will stick around in the neurons of the brain for up to 4-6 weeks after the last dose of the drug (4) which shows how easily we can become addicted, even if we just start off using once a week. Things get even more interesting. Another study was done a couple years later showing that not only does this buildup of Delta FosB occur in the prefrontal cortex, but there is also a slight buildup in our amygdala (5). If you remember in lesson 2, we introduced the amygdala and its reflexive response for self-preservation. With Delta FosB infiltrating the prefrontal cortex, AND the amygdala, not only is it rewiring who you think you are (in the prefrontal cortex which is responsible for awareness), but it is also making you feel like you can't live without it (by affecting the amygdala and its role in self-preservation)! This my friends is the tragic double whammy of addiction – it is a pathological pseudo-education and is why those who are addicted can only think about their next fix. Fortunately, through the rise of neuroplasticity, scientists are finding out that addiction does not damage the brain permanently, so if you do have an addiction to sugar, porn, or your phone, or even some pretty hardcore drugs, we have a few tricks to help you trick the tricksters in your brain.

Sugar Addiction

Dr. Mark Hyman, chairman of the Institute for Functional Medicine, has created a term for a new disorder he calls "diabesity" – which is when people have a combination of type 2 diabetes, and obesity. According to Dr. Hyman this problem is nearing an epidemic as an estimated 35% of Americans have diabesity and millions die each year from complications to being both overweight and diabetic (1). All of this is due to eating sugar. Sugary food, grains, and processed carbohydrates are what we call hyper-rewarding foods. Hyper-rewarding foods (those containing high amounts of salt, fat, and sugar) bypass a negative feedback mechanism in the brain, which tells us we are full, and should not eat anymore. How many times have you been full to the brim, but still had room for that lava cake? Manufacturers know this fact, and by targeting the breakfast industry, keep the general population on a sugar high all day.

The media tells us that kids who eat cereal for breakfast do better in school. First off, cereal should NOT be a breakfast food; it should be a dessert! Even the natural-whole-grain-organic-we-swear-it's-healthy-for-you cereals. What the media, or that heart healthy label doesn't tell you, is that grains in any form are converted in to sugar in the body, and they contain a significant amount of toxins that actually contribute to what is called leaky-gut syndrome, where small particles of food are allowed to pass through your small intestine and into your bloodstream, causing your body to develop an allergic reaction to that food. Fruit and fruit juice is another culprit. I used to love my cereal and juice in the morning as a kid. It was quick, and tasty, but soon I would find myself in school unable to think about anything but food. That's what sugar does to your body; it sends you on a roller coaster of emotions all day long. It breaks your concentration on what is supposed to be priority, and you live every day waiting for your next meal or snack.

Right about now you're probably thinking, "but fruit is good for you, everyone knows that!" One piece of fruit per day is fine, especially if you consume it in the evening. How many pieces of fruit do you think are in your glass of orange juice or apple juice? Not to mention the added sugar as well. People who replace sugar in their diet with fruit because they think it's healthy are only kidding themselves. It causes the same insulin spikes in your body as a candy bar, regardless if there's vitamins in it. Controlling hunger boils down to controlling blood sugar. This is accomplished by eating more healthy fats that occur naturally in food like bacon, beef, coconut, fish, and chicken, followed by fibrous vegetables like broccoli, cauliflower, spinach, celery, cucumber, and zucchini. The maximum amount of meals you should have per day is three (Two is really optimal, with one snack), and if you must have a snack, raw nuts, are your best bet. People who are trying to profit off you will say you need 5-6 meals a day and advocate a low-fat/high-carbohydrate diet. Dr. Barry Sears, creator of the Zone diet, and Dave Asprey, creator of the Bulletproof Diet both agree that if your meal had the proper foods in it, you should not be hungry for 5-7 hours because the food will not only regulate your blood sugar, it will regulate your hormones as well, which is the true demon behind weight gain.

Some very basic supplements you can start taking to help control sugar cravings as you are trying to break this addiction are chromium, Udo's oil, Vitamin D, and Magnesium.

Chromium plays a role in the insulin-signaling pathways that allow our bodies to control the amount of sugar we take in, helping balance blood glucose levels and giving us stable energy. Research also shows that chromium can help protect DNA chromosomes from damage, which means chromium may be able to halt cell mutations that can lead to various chronic diseases (2). The best type to take is Now Foods Tri-Chromium With Cinnamon because it includes Ceylon cinnamon, which is the only cinnamon that helps regulate blood sugar.

Udo's oil is a complete blend of Omega 3 fatty acids that come from a specialized non-destructive extraction process. Your normal oils in the supermarket are damaged from the heating process and also contain bleach, deodorants, and chemicals. You can put Udo's oil on your salads or drizzle a little on your meat when it's out of the oven as this is not oil you cook with; it is oil you consume. Omega 3 fatty acids help curb sugar cravings by providing a greater feeling of satiety after meals. It is also very healthy for your skin, helps build new cells, and maintains brain and nerve function. Start off with one teaspoon after every meal and watch in amazement as this fat restores your health.

Vitamin D actually acts like more of a hormone in your body and is even responsible for regulating several gene expressions in your body. It helps regulate your blood sugar by increasing insulin sensitivity which means sugar is cleared from your blood faster. The best Vitamin D I've found is Sports Research Vitamin D with Organic Coconut Oil. Everyone is deficient in Vitamin D. I don't care where you live, or how much sun you get, you still need to supplement. Taking between 5-15,000 IU's a day will elevate your mood, increase your energy, and boost your immune system as well.

Lastly, magnesium is important to carbohydrate metabolism. It may influence the release and activity of insulin, the hormone that helps control blood glucose levels. Elevated blood glucose levels (like in pre-diabetics) increase the loss of magnesium in the urine, which in turn lowers blood levels of magnesium (3). The only type of magnesium you should take is Ease Magnesium oil, because when you apply magnesium to the skin, it is self-regulating and you don't have to worry about diarrhea if you take too much. 10-20 sprays on your chest and abdomen before you sleep will relax you into getting the best night's sleep of your life, which is important when trying to kick an addiction, especially one like food, because when we don't get enough sleep our body makes more of our hunger hormone, ghrelin, which will cause us to crave sugary foods the next day as well as overeat.

Some people eat to live, while others live to eat. If you're healthy on the outside as well as the inside, then no worries, keep doing what you are doing. For those of you who have health complications related to obesity, this will get you on the right track. Food addiction, not just sugar addiction can cause us to make decisions we regret later on. Regrets combined with unhealthy images of our body breaks several of the rules we talk about when trying to acquire The Everspace. Losing weight, feeling better, and not being controlled by food will allow you to love yourself that much more. If you wish to learn more, check out my book on nutrition The Death of the Diet.

Porn Addiction

I was 18 the first time that I masturbated successfully. Call me a late bloomer or what have you, even though I was attracted to women, I was OBSESSED with sports. Two years later, I was in a steady relationship and having sex regularly. One day I stumbled onto a porn site and this whole magical world was revealed right before my eyes. Now this was the days of dial-up internet, so I was limited to just downloading pictures, but what I noticed was that the more I masturbated to porn, the longer I would last with an actual girl. I never became addicted, but I did have to battle myself from time to time. To be honest, watching the porn was great, but every time I was finished I felt embarrassed and would look back on how silly all of it was. I started to intensely dislike feeling so guilty afterwards, but the urges for it were incredibly distracting and this battle continued for some time. With time, effort (meditation), and knowledge I was able to kick this habit, and today proudly live porn-free.

While watching Internet porn may seem victimless, there are a staggering number of young men who are finding this to be quite the contrary. Ran Gavrieli, a scholar of gender studies in Tel Aviv states that 90% of 12-year-old children are watching porn regularly (6). He says through watching porn, boys grow up learning that sex is about domination rather than it being a sensual loving act. This becomes both addictive and paralyzing, because when it comes time for them to actually relate to another woman, they don't know how, and then revert back to Internet porn. Teenage boys relate what they see on the screen to real life and then go in pursuit of what they consider to be this perfect woman. One teenage boy even admitted he's "ruined the sense of love (7)" through restlessly pursuing women and then getting bored quickly when there is no instant gratification. Digital sex is about being alone, climaxing when you want from what you want. It teaches people that sex is about novelty, that you can have anything you desire (multiple women, multiple positions) in that period of time, but this just isn't how sex is in the real world. Real sex is about connection, love, touching, and INTERACTION. When these boys don't know how to communicate like this, Gavrieli says this starts to mess women up psychologically too because they start to think that in order to deserve love, they need to be sexually desirable so they start dressing and acting the part. When they still aren't received how they imagine, this leads to alcoholism, drug abuse, depression, and in some cases suicide.

Scientists were having a real difficult time studying this because up until 2009, there were no college-age males that were not watching Internet porn regularly (8). In a sense, there was no ability to have a control group which equates to a nearly 100% addiction rate! Compare that to alcohol, which hooks only about 10% of its users and you can see the trouble we are up against. Interestingly, the same rules to addiction apply to Internet porn as they do with drugs, but instead of making you a stud, this type of addiction makes you a dud. Due to this addiction, many males are finding they cannot achieve an erection with a normal woman, even when taking prescription medication for erectile dysfunction. This is because the problem is occurring in the mind, not below the belt. It's not a problem of blood flow; rather it's a problem of brain loss. The hyper-reward Internet porn produces is causing the pleasure center of the brain to short-circuit in real life. This problem becomes two-fold, leaving the man embarrassed, and the woman feeling rejected.

I don't feel I need to convince you this is a problem; some of you may even be experiencing what I am talking about. The way that we neutralize this issue is by learning how to delay gratification. In The Stanford Marshmallow Experiment, psychologist Walter Mischel put children in a room and put a marshmallow in front of them. He told them they had two choices:

1. Eat the marshmallow now
2. Wait 15 minutes and they would get two

What he found was that those children who were able to wait the 15 minutes and delay their gratification got better grades in school, had more ideal bodyweight, and had other more favorable life outcomes (9). Delaying gratification can be done in three different ways. Using "cold" versus "hot" thoughts, happy versus sad thoughts, and associated versus dissociated thoughts. Using these techniques will actually release less dopamine in the brain, allowing you to access your prefrontal cortex to a greater extent where your willpower resides.

- A hot thought is one that arouses, whereas a cold thought is one that is abstract. Rather than thinking about what turns you on in porn, think of how you're viewing it – from a cold lifeless machine running on batteries.
- The brain views sad thoughts much like hot thoughts, which cause you to "miss" something, thus craving the instant gratification of it. To battle this, think of how proud you will be of yourself when you can finally say you've done it; you finally kicked your porn habit.
- Lastly, rather than associating your thoughts with porn making you feel good, use disassociated thought and think about how it must make the women feel. Think about the fact that there are men out there trafficking women for your enjoyment. Think about the lack of value that is being placed on these women. What if that was your daughter, your sister, or a very close friend?

I realize we all have needs and urges, but that doesn't

mean that we always have to act on them. Too much of a good thing can soon become the only thing in this case. Porn undoubtedly turns women into objects, which causes us to reinforce our separateness. I don't know anyone who grows up saying I want to live my life alone with my computer. Alcoholics say your best day drinking, still isn't as good as your worst day sober. The same can be said here, that the best porn video, will never make you feel as good as your worst lover.

Cell Phone Addiction

We all know that one person that is never found to be without their phone. They carry it around tenderly, and maybe wrap it in a bling'd out case. They treat it like a baby, freaking out if it ever goes missing or becomes damaged in any way. This addiction comes from the fact that we see our phone as a travelling reward center. Every ding, pop, or ping lights up our brain and sends dopamine rushing in to see what notification we just got. Did someone like my video? Was it a text? A notification to update an app? According to research (10) 50% of teens say they are addicted to their phone, while 27% of parents say they are addicted to theirs. 69% of parents, and 78% of teens say they check their device hourly. That means that these people cannot sit down and complete a task uninterrupted if it takes longer than an hour. Compare this once again to research showing that 80% of people who try cocaine, are NOT addicted two years later (11). If we can all agree that cocaine is addictive and needs regulation, why aren't we instituting rules for cell phone addiction?

With so many sites making apps and going mobile, this

allows us to stay connect at all times, yet still remain disconnected. We can tell anyone, anything, at any time without really having to talk to them. I see people posting pictures of themselves in the delivery room, while others are writing epitaphs for loved ones that passed away. This stuff used to be communicated face to face, there used to be a connection. We can talk, without talking by using text message, which allows me to respond back to you at the moment of my choosing, or not at all. You can see couples at dinner more interested in their phones than their company. You have people pay money to go to a movie and all the while they are texting or on social media. Cell phones have become the archenemy of the present moment. I realize they're convenient; hell, they may even be able to save a life from time to time, but there's a difference between healthy use and unhealthy use. A difference between convenience and distraction. One college-age woman admitted to sleeping with her phone in her hand (12). This is like an alcoholic sleeping with a bottle of vodka. If someone slept with a bottle of vodka, that's a huge problem, right? But for some reason we feel the phone is harmless even though thousands of studies have shown that cell phone radiation has toxic effects on biological mechanisms in animals from even short-term exposure.

Still don't think your phone is a problem? I remember watching a news report on a woman who was texting while walking out of a store in a Pennsylvania mall and she fell heels over head in a water fountain. She jumped up and quickly walked out of the fountain while looking around if anyone saw her. She was soaked and mall security cameras had caught the whole thing. Someone leaked the footage and the woman ended up suing for damages because she was embarrassed. However, this lady also had a long history of trouble with the law, and was soon to be sentenced for stealing a co-worker's credit card. When all of this came out into the news, she dropped her case. The mall employee who posted the footage ended up getting fired. See what damage can be done from one cell phone incident?

Texting and driving remains to be a serious threat to our roads as well with 64% of all accidents having a phone involved (13). Studies have shown the younger you are, the longer you will look at your phone while driving before thinking you need to look up. As a result, 11 teens die each day in car accidents as a result of texting and driving (14). Cell phone usage is taking people's lives, halting productivity at work, and even inhibiting our ability to walk, but all hope is not lost. There are ways to combat these negative influences brought about by technology so we can have our cake and eat it too.

The first one deals with turning off all of your push notifications. During business hours, keep your phone in a desk drawer, or if you really don't need it for anything, leave it in your car, or in a work locker if you have one. Devote yourself to checking it only on your lunch break, and after work. The excuse, "But what if there's an emergency" is with all due respect, bullshit. How many emergencies have you had in the past week? Month? Year? Ask yourself how bad do you want to make this change.

The second involves turning your phone to a gray scale. Smart phones are made to be appealing to the eye. Notifications are in red because science shows it has an ability to enhance detail. It grabs our attention when it should be elsewhere. To turn an iPhone to gray, go to settings – general – accessibility, and slide the grayscale button over, turning it on. For an Android, it is slightly more complicated, but go to settings – scroll down to about phone – go to build number and tap it several times till it says you have enabled development settings – go back to settings and click on developer options – then go to hardware accelerated rendering – scroll just below to simulate color space – click on that and choose Monochromacy, and you are done!

The third element is to make silent your primary phone setting unless you are waiting for a very important call or text. This allows you to focus better so you are not distracted by miscellaneous texts, or alerts that serve no purpose for what you are doing at the moment.
Lastly, don't sleep with your phone in your bedroom. There are multiple studies, and articles showing proof that the EMF waves, and light from the screen disrupt melatonin levels, which causes you to have a broken sleep pattern during the night, which makes you feel less rested on the same amount of sleep. If you're going to buy an alarm clock, natural light alarm clocks are the way to go. They wake you up naturally with simulated sunlight, which reduces cortisol responses in the body related to traditional beeping, or radio alarm clocks that shock you out of your slumber. Amazon has a plethora of them. A good model will run you between $30 - $50.

Whether you have a family, live with a roommate, or all alone, one of the best practices you can institute, not just for your phone, but when it comes to any technology is to have a power down hour. A power down hour is the hour before bed where you turn off all electronics. You can use this time to meditate, read a book, plan your day tomorrow, journal, or just sit outside and relax.

I hope you now realize the troubles these addictions can cause and how they block you from achieving enough stillness in your life to hear messages from The Everspace. If you have a serious issue with any of the three I mentioned and do not feel like you can change on your own, then seek the help of a friend or a professional. Addiction is challenging to get rid of, and that is why the reward for overcoming it is so great. I understand the challenge of finding your purpose in life, but to never find it, let alone even get the chance to question it, is one of the greatest tragedies we can ever face. There's hope for everyone, you just have to want it.

A Guide to Self-Awareness

"The intuitive mind is a sacred gift and the rational mind is a faithful servant. We have created a society that honors the servant and has forgotten the gift."

-A. Einstein

In the movie, A Bronx Tale (15), Sonny, a gangster, takes a liking to a boy who lives close to his bar named Calogero. Sonny shot a man in broad daylight and Calogero was a witness. Even though he was only maybe 6 or 7 years old at the time, he idolized Sonny and understood he had to lie to the police when they asked him if Sonny was indeed the killer. As Calogero grows up, Sonny allows him to do odd jobs for him to make money and sort of looks after Calogero like a second father. One day when Calogero expresses his ambition to be a gangster like Sonny, he reprimands him, telling him not to do what he does. When Calogero asks why, Sonny says, "The saddest thing in life is wasted talent," and I tend to agree.

We all have a talent or a passion, and we have a responsibility to our soul to realize it in our lifetime. How do you know what yours is though? Bill Harris, author of The New Science of Super Awareness (16) says that when it comes to figuring out your purpose in life, "Knowing is like the boobie prize in personal growth." The key is awareness. Awareness is not a knowing, it is not a consciousness, it is deeper than that and more profound. It's an understanding we are all born with and we all have the ability to manifest this understanding. The reason why most people never find their purpose, become stuck, or feel lost in life is because of the two main keys we already discussed. What your beliefs are (selective consciousness), and what you put your attention into to (distractions, or addictions). If you put headphones on and blast music in every class, you may know some of the material for the test, but likely not enough to pass any of the tests. This is what our life becomes like when we are told what to believe, and live our life with so many distractions.

Harris describes how all of our feelings actually stem from choices we have made. However, if we do not have a high level of awareness, it will seem like events in our life just happen, and we then react to them. We become angry, or sad, and contend that things are out of our control. He says, "It will seem as if the situation caused the feelings, when actually it's what you did in response to the situation that actually created the feelings. Seen with awareness, however, your response, and the resulting feelings, would become a choice." It seems we only do things that do not serve us when we do them outside of our awareness. When we do this, we are not paying attention to life. We are distracted. When we develop enough awareness however, we are more conscious to choose what serves us and everything else just falls by the wayside. It is at this point that we start to feel guided by life. Life turns extremely fortuitous and all worries, all fear simply start to fade away. We, in a sense, become self-realized.

Statistics show that only 2% of people actually take action on what they want to do. The rest of us fall in line in the rat race, fearful of striking it out on our own. We are brought up and become accustomed to a life of certainty, but to strike your own path you must move from a position of faith. Bill Harris says it is the price we pay for not having enough awareness. Life is lived through choices we make every day. Choice occurs in the prefrontal cortex of our brain, the same area affected by addiction. When that area is distracted by thoughts of sex, food, drugs, our cell phone, or even what we have to do for the rest of the day, this inhibits the amount of awareness we have and decreases the amount choices we "think" we have available. Rather than take action towards what we really want, we sit back and wish for it to happen. I wish I had this talent, or this car, or that house. If you're religious you may pray for it, but God doesn't work like this. God is a creator. Rather than ask for a hand out, ask God to co-create with you. Ask for guidance or direction, and tell him you're willing to do all of the work necessary.

When it comes to choice, Harris says we only have three categories. 1) Things you have no choice about. 2) Things you can influence. 3) Things you could have a choice about. That you only have a choice about what you create, but you also have to have enough awareness to realize you can create it. He goes on to say we can only create four things: How we feel, how we behave, what we attract, and the meanings we assign to what happens. You can see now why throughout this book we have been trying to cultivate a sense of positivity, connectedness, love, acceptance and understanding. By instituting these character traits, we can in a sense "bend" reality. We can make the world what we want. It can either be a perfect bountiful setting on which we do our work to help others, and ourselves, or it can be an unfair, God-forsaken hell hole with the slogan, "Life's a bitch." How do we create this awareness? The technique is simple and has been around for thousands of years. You may remember I foreshadowed this technique two chapters back, if you don't, you need to increase your awareness! The way we do that is through meditation.

Cultivating Awareness Through Meditation

Meditation, to most people is a silly exercise to "stop thinking", or "clear your head." This is actually what meditation is not. Meditation is about observation and change. The first time I meditated, I went to a silent retreat in Assisi, Italy in October of 2015. I was a one-hit wonder. I sat down the first time and didn't move for over an hour and a half. I was amazed by how I felt after and immediately realized the benefits. Determined, I sat down the next morning and dealt with a lot of discomfort. I could feel tension in my left leg and my right arm, which forced me to consciously relax those areas, thus breaking myself out of meditation. My mind was flooded with silly thoughts that kept distracting me. When the hour was up I walked out of the room more frustrated than when I walked in it. After 5 days of meditation, I left determined to keep the practice going, but when I got home, I fell back into my same old routine.

In February of 2016 I wanted to take my business, and my life to the next level so I bought into a mastermind group called The Edge 100 Brotherhood. After passing the interviews to see if I was the right fit for the program, I logged into my account online to watch the first video that I had missed a couple days back. After a short introduction, Raul, the creator of the program says the first thing we are going to do in the morning is get up and do what he calls the "Ritual." It's a meditation, combined with NLP (Neuro Linguistic Programming). "Oh great," I said to myself, here we go again. The next morning, with my headphones set, I woke up 30 minutes earlier than normal and did this Ritual. To my surprise, 10 minutes into it, I'm sobbing like a little baby who just got his favorite toy taken away. The meditation was only 20 minutes long. It turns out that there are active, and passive ways to meditate. The passive way is what I consider going from tee-ball to the big leagues overnight. Being still is impossible for some people at the beginning. The active way of meditating allows beginners to harness the power of distraction to improve their meditation. As I meditated more and more this way, my sadness soon turned into an intense power radiating in my body. Rather than having thoughts about fried chicken or when I'm going to play video games next, some very, very deep insights were flooding my brain. At points, I would run from the back of my gym up to the desk to write down what I was receiving. Sometimes, in the middle of class even. Needless to say, this form of meditation changed me and it changed my life. Being curious, and a scientist, I took to researching the direct cause of action behind all of this and what I found absolutely fascinated me.

Neuroplasticity

Scientists used to believe that once you reached a certain age, the brain no longer made changes. With new research, we are finding out that the brain is in fact plastic. It can be molded through the course of our lifetime and will produce new neurons every time we learn something new. Scientists call this neuroplasticity, or brain plasticity. Remember Delta FosB? That's one of the mechanisms of neuroplasticity. It seems that the brain is pretty smart and realizes when we are learning something of value for the organism so it starts sending out signals causing it to change. The great news is the stimulus doesn't have to be a drug, or a dopamine response for this to kick into gear. This can happen by learning a language, a complex motor skill like golf, and best of all, it happens through meditation!

It turns out that when you focus your mind on something, you actually cause your brain wave patterns to fire in slow motion. Think about it: when you're learning to ride a bike, you don't take your first trip down a steep hill do you? You start off slowly, and with more wheels even. The brain is the same way. As we are learning slowly on the outside, the brain is learning slowly on the inside to get things just right. To do this, your brain produces electrical impulses from your neurons that fire rhythmically to produce what we call brain waves. Brain waves are precursors to our thoughts, emotions, and total body well-being, and there are four types we need to be concerned with.

Beta waves when firing slowly are helping you focus or increase your ability to concentrate. When Beta waves get excited though, they produce arousal and anxiety. These are the primary brain waves we use in our day-today life. Since meditation slows this type of brain wave, it is one reason those who meditate are happier and less stressed, or can handle stressful situations better.

Alpha waves are a little slower than Beta, and are primarily firing when you wake up. They also occur when you are in a state of deep relaxation. Ever get sucked into a good book (maybe this one??) and have time blow by? Your Alpha waves were firing to help increase your ability to learn, process, store, and then recall the information. People who meditate make more of these brain waves even when they are not meditating.

Theta brain waves are slower than both Beta and Alpha and enhance our ability to create. It's not just art either. When we are formulating new connections to things, or solving a problem with an Ah-Ha moment, your brain is producing massive amounts of Theta waves. Theta waves also enhance your ability to learn and turns your brain into a proverbial sponge for information. You guessed it, meditators make more of this brain wave as well. The more Theta waves you produce, the greater your ability is to experience profound amounts of joy or bliss (Hmmmm, did we talk about this already?). It takes time though, and is a great reward for those who are consistent.

Delta waves are the slowest waves our brains make. Enhanced Delta waves correlate to increased abilities to lead, and persuade others. They are also very active in our deepest stages of sleep when we are said to be completely unconscious. It is no wonder that high amounts of waking Delta waves increase our feeling of oneness with the world. When Delta waves are firing, our body releases anti-aging properties like growth hormone, and also allows us to tap into our intuition easier. Deep meditative experiences like those of monks increase Delta waves, which literally alter consciousness during the time of meditation. This means highly spiritual occurrences like out-of-body, or near-death experiences.

The benefits meditation provides our brain waves can be summed up in two words – increased awareness. Remember, awareness is NOT knowing. It's not an intellect per se. It's a flow state that enhances your knowledge the way a wide-angled lens can increase the confines of a picture. Awareness allows us to access the big picture of our life. It erases the feeling of "I'll never be anything, or do anything with my life." Most of us grow up struggling to find a purpose in life because we don't apply techniques like meditation that increase our awareness which open up our ability to create, as well as expand the choices that we have. Tony Robbins says, "Most people don't live the life of their dreams, they live their conditioning." Which is to say, we live according to what other people tell us we are supposed to do. Conditioning is why people scoff at Tim Ferriss' 4 Hour Work Week, or any other resource that challenges the "Normal" way of thinking. Incredibly, with the information on brain waves, we have only scratched the surface of what meditation can do for our being. In Dan Harris' book 10% Happier (17) he talks about what he considers to be an almost laughable laundry list of benefits from thousands of studies, which include but are not limited to:

* Helping major depression
* Drug addiction
* Binge eating
* Smoking cessation
* Decreased stress among cancer patients

* Decreased loneliness among senior citizens
* ADHD
* Asthma
* Psoriasis
* Irritable bowel syndrome

The health benefits are irrefutable, yet are beyond the scope of this book. We are primarily concerned with the benefits produced in the brain. Consistent meditation has also been found to enhance what is called whole brain thinking. Remember how I said in lesson 4 that our brain has two halves and is connected by a thick bridge of tissue? Meditation enhances the ability of both sides to talk to each other. This once again helps increase the amount of awareness we can have at any given moment. Your ability to think and provide answers to problems is greatly enhanced. Bill Harris says, "Awareness provides an answer to all human problems that don't have a solution." Not sure what job to take? Awareness to the rescue! Not sure if you should date that girl? Awareness to the rescue! Can't decide where to go on vacation? Awareness to the rescue! This is what it means to be living in The Everspace. A faster and wider range of solutions available to you at a moment's notice, a greater amount of creativity to enhance the productivity of your life's work, and a calmer more focused demeanor by which to operate from.

There are many different ways for people to meditate. You can focus on your breath, repeat a mantra, chant and perform specialized breathing, and even sit and focus on cloud formations in the sky. In my experience, each one is unique and offers good variety to keep you interested, but is most beneficial when done with a guide or teacher. Like I said earlier, I feel active meditation is best for the beginner. It allows you to repeat something, or listen to music, which causes a distraction to distract you from your thinking mind.

For the general population, I would like to recommend Bill Harris' program called Holosync. I still do my ritual every day, but after close to a year found myself wanting to meditate for a longer period of time. I wanted to go deeper and reach another level and this did the trick. Holosync is an audio program that makes meditating fun, and easy, plus I know a lot of people like to make time an excuse for not being able to meditate. Using Holosync provides a great solution for that since all you have to do is wake up 30 minutes earlier than you usually do, roll over, put your headphones on and then lay back and listen. If you fear falling back to sleep (the chimes are set to rain falling in the background) simply set your timer or alarm on your phone as well. What about being more tired throughout the day? That's a half hour of sleep I may lose! Meditation actually gives you more energy for your day. When solutions come faster and clearer you will waste less energy trying to figure something out, as well as trying to remember what important tasks you have to accomplish during the day, plus, like studies show it reduces the amount of stress we feel and stress is a massive energy drainer! I actually feel less tired now that I meditate, and my normal bedtime has gone from 10:30pm to almost midnight!

Holosync is backed by years of research and over two million happy customers; that is what drew me to this product. I am also living proof that it even helped me and continues to help me even though I was already a seasoned meditator. Through a half hour of listening to this technology, your brain gains a feeling of meditating for

228

close to 8 hours! Without trying to sound like a commercial, I highly suggest you try it – you will not be disappointed. Bill also has plenty of available upgrades once Holosync's magic starts to slow down. The original program is good for 6 months of benefits, and in some cases can last for up to a year before you need a more powerful stimulus to take your brain waves deeper. To try it out free of charge go to www.centerpointe.com.

For male entrepreneurs looking for a little more of a challenge, I highly recommend Raul Villacis and his Next Level Experience. If I had to pinpoint one thing that changed my life in 2016, it would be this program. It's a little bit bigger of a buy in, and you have to go through a few interviews in which you will be forced to have some pretty tough conversations, but once you're in, the potential of your business, your being, your body, and your bonds will skyrocket. This program has too many benefits to list, like weekly calls from Raul himself, to group challenges that help you expand your business consciousness, as well as retreats he organizes if you are looking to level up even further. Access to the closed Facebook group is worth the price of admission alone. It is the equivalent of being able to communicate with other men who are doing the same meditation as you, and being able to gain their insights as well. Not to mention Raul posts some insightful gems in there from time to time. A word of caution, this group is not for the faint of heart, nor is it a turnstile that people pass in and out of. This is a commitment you are making, and you will be called out on your shit if you do not put in the work. Since February of 2016, I think 4 men who were added have been able to stay in the group. The rest left within a week. To set the ball rolling on this one, visit http://nextlevelexperience.com.

For female entrepreneurs (did you think I was going to forget about you?) I highly recommend Marisa Peer's program Uncompromised Life from Vishen Lakhiani's Mindvalley Academy. Marisa works with the top 1% of super-achievers in the world and specializes in hypnosis. Her ideas are revolutionary and understand how to get to the core of what in your mind is holding you back from success. Her hypnotic section on "The Healing Vortex" once again is worth the price tag alone. Hypnosis has a lot of the same benefits meditation does and has been shown to ease the discomfort of hot flashes. Marisa's voice is very soothing, so I suggest listening to her informational video on each section during your morning commute, then the hypnosis portion before you go to sleep. It's an 8-week course so you'll be doing the same hypnosis every night for 7 days. To learn more, go to http://courses.mindvalleyacademy.com/uncompromised-life/.

To leave you, I'd like to use the words of someone wiser than myself. It's something I live by and read whenever I need the proverbial "Reality check."

"Man, you have been a citizen of this great World-City! Whether for five years or fifty, what does it matter? Its laws are the same for all men. What grounds have you to complain? You are not banished from the City by a tyrant or unjust judge, but by the same nature that settled you in the City. You are no different from the actor who is dismissed from a play by the director who hired him. "But I have played only three acts, not five!" Well said, but your life's drama is complete in three acts. **He who once caused your composition and now calls for your dissolution determines the moment of completion. These are not your decisions. Make a graceful exit**

then, worthy of the grace you have been shown."

-Marcus Aurelius

Your Key to Accessing The Everspace: Meditation

I seriously can't emphasize it enough. Meditate. Meditate. Meditate. Everything that came to me in this book was a result first and foremost from meditation. I institute every lesson in this book every day and it has changed my life remarkably. Worry is down 98%. Negativity is non-existent. Judgment is gone, and I even look at people's imperfections as beautiful. There are some people that can make it to the top by being an asshole, but for the rest of us we need greater mental space and clarity. We don't want to live in a dog-eat-dog world.

If you're like me, there are a million excuses running through your head right now. Kyle Cease has a 2-day personal growth conference he teaches called Evolving Out Loud. His slogan? Show up and stay in the room! That's what I want you to do. Sit or lie in a room and stay there for a period of time. Don't worry about what is going on in your brain, just observe how funny, sick, and twisted it all is. If you decide to invest in one of the programs, great, I have full confidence they will help each and every one of you. If you want to go it alone to test the waters, that's great too. There is no right or wrong when it comes to meditation, there's only right for you, and I encourage you to keep trying things till something sticks and your mind gets blown – literally.

231

Uncomfortability Challenge

You had to know this was coming. Even though meditation is becoming more mainstream, there is still a stigma behind it that meditators are weird, fairy-loving flower children. My challenge to you then is to find someone to meditate with to show others you can meditate and be completely normal without joining a cult or moving to India. Once is enough, but if you want to keep trying to get multiple people to do it then more power to you!

Are You Looking To Go Deeper?
There are very few books written in such a way that it will actually change someone's life. While I did my best with this one, sometimes knowledge isn't enough for us to take action. If you would like to invest in your personal development further, please consider my online course at www.attitude-love-gratitude.com.

References

1. http://drhyman.com/blog/2015/07/16/why-skinny-fat-can-be-worse-than-obesity/
2. https://draxe.com/what-is-chromium/
3. http://healing.about.com/od/dietandfitness/a/magnesiumfacts_3.htm
4. Nestler, E. J. (2005). Is there a common molecular pathway for addiction? Nature Neuroscience, 8(11), 1445-1449. Doi:10.1038/nn1578
5. Perrotti, L., Weaver, R., Robison, B., Renthal, W., Maze, I., Yazdani, S., . . . Nestler, E. (2008). Distinct patterns of ?fosB induction in brain by drugs of abuse. Synapse, 62(5), 358-369. Doi:10.1002/syn.20500
6. T. (2013). Why I stopped watching porn | Ran Gavrieli | TEDxJaffa. Retrieved December 03, 2016, from http://www.youtube.com/watch?v=gRJ_QfP2mhU
7. InRealLife. (n.d.). Retrieved December 05, 2016, from http://dogwoof.com/inreallife
8. T. (2012). The great porn experiment | Gary Wilson | TEDxGlasgow. Retrieved December 05, 2016, from http://www.youtube.com/watch?v=wSF82AwSDiU
9. Stanford marshmallow experiment. (n.d.). Retrieved December 05, 2016, from https://en.wikipedia.org/wiki/Stanford_marshmallow_experiment
10. Dealing with Devices: The Parent-Teen Dynamic | Common Sense Media. (n.d.). Retrieved December 05, 2016, from https://www.commonsensemedia.org/technology-addiction-concern-controversy-and-finding-balance-infographic
11. H. (n.d.). Understanding Cocaine Addiction. Retrieved December 05, 2016, from https://www.verywell.com/cocaine-addiction-4014455

12. Are we addicted to the Internet? – CNN Video. (n.d.). Retrieved December 05, 2016, from http://edition.cnn.com/videos/tech/2015/06/18/digital-dependence-kelly-wallace-social-media-cell-phones-orig.cnn

13. The 25 Scariest Texting and Driving Accident Statistics. (2015). Retrieved December 05, 2016, from http://www.icebike.org/texting-and-driving/

14. Texting and Driving Statistics – Distracted Driving Drives Up Risk. (n.d.). Retrieved December 06, 2016, from https://www.edgarsnyder.com/car-accident/cause-of-accident/cell-phone/cell-phone-statistics.html

15. De Niro, R. (Director), De Niro, R. (Producer), & Palminteri, C. (Writer). (n.d.). A Bronx tale [Video file].

16. Harris, B. (2015). The New Science Of Super Awareness. Beaverton, Oregon: Centerpointe Press.

17. Harris, D. (2014). 10% happier: How I tamed the voice in my head, reduced stress without losing my edge, and found self-help that actually works: A true story. New York, NY: It Books, an imprint of HarperCollins.

Epilogue

I would like to take this time to thank you, the reader for embarking on this journey with me. Whether it was the book cover, the name, or divine intervention, it matters not. This book was presented to you when it was supposed to. As I was writing this I was travelling through Europe, staying in Airbnb's, and each host was inquisitive as to what brought me to their place. When I told them I was writing a book they all wanted to know what it was about. What I found interesting was that my description of what I was writing never changed, and neither did the reaction of my host. I told them I was trying to bridge the gap between God and science; that what science can't explain, God can, and what God promises to be real, science is slowly catching on to. After saying that, their faces would zone out in deep thought for about 5 seconds, and when they came back to the present they would say, "That sounds very interesting."

Ultimately, this was a calling. Some stories in this book I remembered from glancing at a TV screen in 2004. It remained dormant for twelve years and then resurfaced when I needed it to make a connection. How do you explain that? You don't. There are three things I would like you to take away from this book. The first is to stop trying to explain everything in your life. Trust that it happened for a reason and move forward faithfully, knowing you are going to grow from the is-ness of it. The second is to live by relative truth. If it makes you happy, and is not hurting anyone, don't listen to the haters. You will never burden others by what is true, same as living in non-truths will burden both you and others. On a long enough timeline people see through everyone's bullshit, and being exposed is much harder to handle than being honest.

Lastly, never stop feeling how small you are. Consider this fact: The Sloan Great Wall is a group of galaxies that form a string (also called a galactic filament) held together by dark matter. The size? Only 1.37 billion light years across. It is 1/60th of the observable Universe. Light can travel 5.88 trillion miles in a single year. I tried to multiply 5.88 trillion by 1.37 billion and my calculator took a hike. The point of all this? Life is too precious to be anything but happy. In order to change the world you live in, you first have to change your mind and the way you perceive any and all life situations. The phrase "Life is too short" is not meant to be a statement of measurement, but a statement about quality. It is to say life is too short not to tell a family member you love them. Life is too short to not bury the hatchet in a pointless dispute about who took out the trash last. Life is too short to not use your time productively, rather than foolishly. My earlier years used to be filled with all of this pessimism, and now all of that has been switched over to complete and utter hope. While some say hope may make a man crazy, pessimism doesn't keep you warm on a single night. If you put the lessons in this book into practice, I can guarantee this same profound, yet simple shift will occur in you. Your parents will notice. Your friends will notice.

And most importantly, God will notice.

All my best,

CK
December 9th, 2016
Göttingen, Germany

Acknowledgements

I would like to send a huge thank you to Dan Hoar and Andrea Palomo. I'm sure you didn't realize it at the time, but our conversations about life were helping me infinitely more than they were helping you. The corny side of me tends to believe we are soul mates; if you're OK with it, then so am I.

To Adam Payne, a huge thank you for introducing me to Alan Watts. You always expressed your value for my newsletters, Alan Watts provided a lot of value for me, and that was all because of you.

To Teresa and Steve Martindale, your support through my business endeavors has been unwavering to the point that it will probably take me a few lifetimes to pay you back, but I'll do it somehow, probably when you least expect it.
Last, but never least, at least in a learned man's heart, I'd like to thank Tony Ward for introducing me to Son of Citation which saved me probably four days, and a lot of boredom when citing my work.

Get In Touch With Me!

TWITTER - @chriskidawski

FACEBOOK – Christopher J. Kidawski

http://www.downloadingdaily.com

Want Free Books?

I'm giving away three free books if you are interested. These books have been highly influential in my development as a human being and all of them come in kindle format for your convenience. Type the following link into your browser and please consider signing up: http://downloadingdaily.com/books/three-free-books/

Made in the USA
Middletown, DE
24 February 2018